Making Make-Believe

Other Books by MaryAnn F. Kohl

Action Art with Barbara Zaborowski

Discovering Great Artists with Kim Solga

Good Earth Art with Cindy Gainer

Great American Artists for Kids with Kim Solga

Mudworks

Mudworks, Bilingual Edition

Science Arts with Jean Potter

Scribble Art

Storybook Art with Jean Potter

Making Make-Believe

Hands-on Projects for Play and Pretend

MaryAnn F. Kohl

Dedication

In memory of Roy Rogers, King of the Cowboys

The author as a young cowgirl.

Published by Chicago Review Press Incorporated
814 North Franklin Street
Chicago, Illinois 60610
ISBN 978-0-914090-48-9

Cover design: Jonathan Hahn
Cover photograph: Choreograph/iStock

Printed in the United States of America
5 4 3 2 1

Cataloging-in-Publication Data is available from the Library of Congress

Table of Contents

Using the Icons

Experience level

Use the experience icon to choose a project, based on how easy or difficult it might be.

★ one star for the beginning artist with little experience

★★ two stars for artists with some art experience

★★★ three stars for the more experienced artist

Remember that age and skill do not necessarily go hand-in-hand. Although the activities in *Making Make-Believe* are geared toward children between the ages of three and eight, older children may enjoy them without the same level of adult assistance.

Planning and preparation

The planning and preparation icons show how easy or difficult it is to prepare for the activity.

1 all materials are likely to be found in the home or school.

2 all materials are familiar but may need to be found or purchased before beginning the activity.

3 requires materials that may be unfamiliar, but easily gotten.

Techniques

Many projects incorporate more than one art medium; the icon shows the primary one.

 painting

 drawing

 game

 sculpture

 just hands

 scissors

tape, glue, etc.

 weaving

 sewing

 cooking

Put some make-believe into your life!

Making Make-Believe is filled with over 125 rich ideas for simple, creative play and pretend activities for children. The book is both a motivational idea book and a rich resource of ideas for pretending and dramatic play with children. Making make-believe has never been so much fun or so easy.

Making Make-Believe has seven chapters that describe dramatic play activities, from simple play settings to puppets, from costumes and props to storybook ideas. Each idea is illustrated to highlight that project. Each project has icons at the top corner of the page to help the reader evaluate the project as to type of project, time needed to prepare, and ease of use. The table of contents is a good place to find the ideas arranged in their chapter groupings. Browsing the index offers the reader another venue for finding ideas arranged and grouped by materials and props, or alphabetically by project name.

Use this book to stimulate children's creative play. The purpose of *Making Make-Believe* is to encourage children to develop their imaginations naturally, with only a small amount of help from adults. This is a book to enjoy and use all year long, at home or at school, in a kitchen or in a classroom, inside and out!

What things are needed for making make-believe?

All you need are a few props and materials and an area where children can play comfortably. Use what you have on hand rather than providing every material suggested in each activity. Children can gather their own props, or adults can help them. Some basic props are cardboard boxes, dolls, blocks, and dress-up clothes in all kinds of career and role themes. Simple organization ideas include using prop boxes labeled "Housekeeping Box," "Fairy Tale Box," "Post Office Box," and so on. Keep clothing on racks or pegs; use shelves, shoeboxes, and plastic trays to organize things.

What kind of space is right for pretend play?

Here, there, and everywhere! Pretend play is appropriate wherever it is permissible, from a pile of blocks to a puppet stage, from a hallway to under a table, from outdoors to indoors.

What do make-believe, pretend, and dramatic play have in common?

The terms make-believe, pretend, and dramatic play all mean the same thing—children using their imaginations to play. We have all heard children say things like "Let's play house," "Let's pretend that we're the king and queen of all the woods," or "Look at me! My trike is the fastest rocket ship in the sky." When children act as part of their play, it is called dramatic play. A few examples of typical dramatic play are House, Tea Party, Firefighter, Dolls, and Trucks. Some children may even pretend they are dogs or cats for days on end, or confront their fears by pretending to be superheroes fighting nighttime monsters. Children will also take on the roles of adults in their lives, by pretending to be mothers and fathers, doctors, rock stars, or astronauts. They frequently play the roles of imaginary characters like queens, fairies, aliens, or storybook friends.

What is the adult's role in dramatic play?

The adult helps gather the props and materials, and assists with cutting and difficult gluing or sewing. But the adult is mostly an observer of children's play, keeping an eye on what further materials might be gathered or mixed into the play. The adult can sometimes join in for a cup of tea, be the knock at the door, or participate briefly in some other way to help the children refine, extend, or elaborate play. Often adults can join in just long enough to give the play a nudge forward, or boost the level of play to a more complex level, but always following the children's lead.

At what ages do children enjoy making make-believe?

Around 1½ children begin pretending with toy trucks, dolls, and tea parties with mommy and daddy. By age four or five their play is much more intricate, and they are greatly inspired by props and everyday life experiences. Some children will keep imaginative play going through age ten or so, often playing alone with toys or props at home, and then blending their imaginations into activities such as school plays, creative writing, music, and art.

What about weapons, superheroes, and power play?

This type of play is natural and normal, and lets children pretend they have control over their lives and fears. As a superhero, the child is becoming a powerful person who can conquer anything. If children's play becomes too powerful, violent, or scripted, the adult can re-direct the children to another play idea. Of course, all children should feel safe and no child should ever be allowed to hurt others.

How does dramatic play help children develop?

All areas benefit from dramatic play. Some examples are:

Cognitive—children solve problems like who gets to be the wolf, or what to use as a prop for a magic wand. Language develops as children use sentences and phrases to direct the pretending and communicate with each other. Children may also learn to understand symbolic thinking such as mime or using imaginary props.

Emotional—pretending is the perfect time for children to express emotions and to learn to be in control of their own play. It is a time to work through stressful or happy occasions. It is a time to let fantasy and reality blend without the worry of which is which.

Social—playing and pretending with others is a time to learn how to get along, share roles, cooperate, and work through problems. Role-playing is a chance for children to "try on" the roles of people in their lives, like a baby sister, parent, or teacher, or roles from their imaginations, like dinosaurs and firefighters.

Creative—creativity blossoms and grows through pretending and dramatic play. The children use their imaginations to steer play, to control it with rules and guides, and to make use of props and accessories in new and wonderful ways. And only they have the power to undo, redo, or create their play situations.

Physical—all of the many things children do as part of their play will help develop fine and large motor skills, which will later help them do things like cut with scissors, hold a pencil, jump rope, or write their names.

Dramatic play, pretend, and make-believe are an important part of the proper development of all children, a natural and wonderful part of growing that can be enhanced by adults fortunate enough to be included in the circles of children. To encourage dramatic play is to encourage happy, healthy child development.

Encourage the making of make-believe. It is one of the most naturally satisfying times of childhood, and one of the most valuable. Play is learning; learning is play.

Acknowledgments

I would like to acknowledge, with great thanks and respect, the following educators from my e-mail sharing groups who have contributed their dramatic play and pretend ideas to this book. Although most of us have never met, I feel we have developed lasting friendships through our sharing, and I look forward to meeting each and every one sometime in the future. My deepest thanks to all of these contributors.

A. Wilson, BC, Canada
Aleen Dean, CA
Anette Whelan, Western Australia
Ann Scalley, MA
Barbara Zager, NJ
Berni Kirkpatrick, OR
Carmen Martin, WI
Cate Heroman, LA
Cathy-Dee Bran, AL, Canada
Charlene Woodham Peace, AL
Cheryl Joyce, NY
Elanie Rogers, OR
Gail Hariton, NY
Jane Armstrong, AZ
Jane Harris, IL
Judi Woodards, OH
Judy Gorham, MA
Kandi Cohen, NY
Kaye Williams, UT
Kimberly Torretti, TX
Laura Gaxxano, MA
Lisa Layton, MO
Loreen McDonald
Lynn Coleman, NY
Marla Landis, MA
Melanie Young, TX
Michelle Marie Pena, CA
Nicole Vig, WI
Pam Nesmith Beard, VA
Peg Romanelli, IL
Peta Wells, Western Australia
Richard Karch, CA
Sandy Rivarola, South Africa
Sharon Botsford, KS
Shaynee Stevens, CA
Shelly Cummings, TX
Stefanie Hoover, KS
Sue Obee, BC, Canada
Suzi Chase, AZ
Terri Bose, NY
Vicki Crandell, IN
Zanni Van Antwerp, CA

The author is seated on the top row, she is second from the left.

Play Settings & Imagination Spaces

Chapter 1

1

Simple Things Are Best

SIMPLE PROPS AND EASY PLAY EXPERIENCES ARE OFTEN BEST, REQUIRING LITTLE OF ADULTS AND EVOKING THE MOST NATURAL, REFRESHING, IMAGINATIVE RESPONSES FROM CHILDREN.

Autumn Leaves

- Rake leaves into pathways and trails, creating rooms and hallways for play.

Blankets, Sheets, and Towels

- Blankets, sheets, and towels are wonderful materials to inspire imaginative and creative play. They can be anything: a superhero's cape, the sails for a ship, a cozy cover for a doll in the hospital, the walls of a magical castle, the throne of a queen.

Blocks

- Wooden blocks or plastic blocks; homemade blocks or store bought blocks; big blocks or little blocks. Blocks to build with, sit on, drive, or fly. Blocks for doll furniture, or homes for gerbils. Blocks, blocks, blocks are perfect for motivating creative thinking and play. You can never have enough blocks!

Boxes

- Cardboard boxes of all shapes and sizes—large and small, wide and narrow, tall and short—can become forts, treasure boxes, cradles, cars, a scientific laboratory, or a tidy school room. Collect and save them for play, and when done, recycle them!

Cardboard

- Cardboard cut into a frame that fits the face of a child can become a television screen, framed artwork, window, or computer monitor.

LEAF HOUSE

CAPE (TOWEL)

Furniture

- Use cushions or pillows to make a pirate ship. Have a tea party in a fairy glen under a table. Build a bridge with a wooden chair for the Billy Goats Gruff.

Indoors or Out.

- Move typical indoor activities outside and traditional outdoor activities inside for an all new imaginative kick-start!

Pebbles, Pine Cones, and Acorns

- Add a few pebbles to the sand pile, use pine cones to make a house where acorn-people live. Pebbles, rocks, pine cones, acorns, weeds, leaves, bark, dirt, mud, sand, and grasses are just of few of the things children can play with indoors or out.

Sand Box

- Add containers, tools, dishes, plastic pipes, a hose and water, toys, or bare feet and bathing suits. Each addition becomes a new ingredient to stimulate creative play in imaginative new ways.

Water

- Water in the sink, in the grass, in the sand box, in a puddle, in the tub, in a bucket—wherever you have water, you have imaginative play.

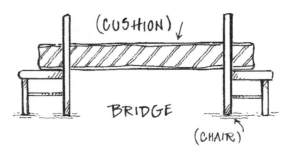

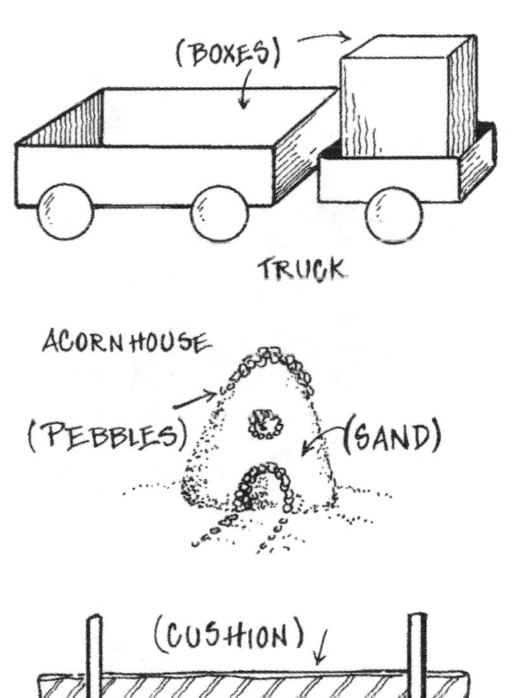

1 Old Sheet Play Table

CONVERT AN OLD SHEET DRAPED OVER A CARD TABLE INTO A HOUSE, COTTAGE, CABIN, CAVE, FORT, OR OTHER IMAGINATIVE PLACE.

Materials

old sheet
card table, or any sturdy table
crayons or markers
scissors
clothespins or books, optional
large safety pins, diaper pins, or clothespins

Steps

- Begin by draping an old sheet over a card table. Position the sheet evenly over the table. Trim the excess while the sheet is hanging. If necessary, hold the sheet in place with clothespins or books placed on top.
- Fold the extra sheet material at each corner. Use large safety pins to hold. The extra sheet can also be trimmed.
- To make windows, draw an H on one of the walls. Cut along the lines of the H. Use safety pins to hold the window open. Make windows on three sides, but leave room for a door on one side.
- To make a door, draw an upside down L with the straight leg of the L touching the floor. Cut along the lines of the L for a door that will open. Again, use safety pins to hold the door opened or closed.
- Climb inside the play zone and imagine it is a cabin, cottage, playhouse, cave, fort, or other imaginative play area.

More Ideas

After the sheet is cut to fit, remove it from the card table and spread it on the floor. Use fabric paint, fabric crayons, or regular crayons to decorate the play zone. Glue on fabric, felt, and sewing trim to add features like a doorknob, flowers, shutters, faucet, mailbox, or other exterior house ideas. Then put the sheet back on the table.

An old tablecloth, thin bedspread, or blanket will work instead of a sheet.

Blanket Land

10

Transform tables, chairs, pillows, boxes, or furniture into an imaginative pretend place called "Blanket Land."

Materials

blankets, sheets, or other large lightweight fabrics, such as
beach towel • large piece of fabric • old drapes or curtains • old sheet • thin bedspread
furniture or boxes, such as
big pillows and cushions • cardboard boxes • chairs • sofa • stools, hassock • tables
extra items for pretend, such as
books • flashlight • paper and crayons • sleeping bag • stuffed animals
helpful building supplies, optional, such as
clothespins • masking or duct tape • string or rope
toys of all kinds

Steps

- Assemble the blankets or other fabrics. Choose an area with sturdy furniture to incorporate in the building and play.
- Spread a blanket out over some chairs. Look inside and see what you think about the space.
- Join more chairs and maybe a table to support more blankets for a larger "land." Build Blanket Land as big or small as you wish. Use clothespins, tape, or string to make Blanket Land secure and sturdy.
- Choose books, toys, pets, snacks, pillows, and other items to enjoy inside the structure. A flashlight can add extra fun.

More Ideas

Take sheets and blankets outside with a basket of clothespins for children to create their own structures and "lands."

Think about spending the night or taking a nap in Blanket Land!

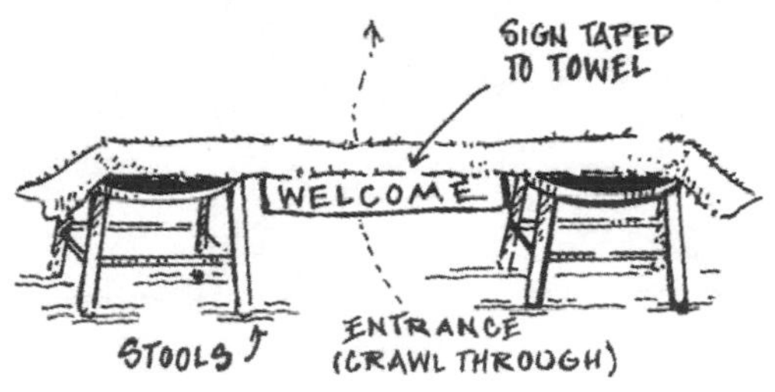

1 GLUE

Newspaper Play Space

BUILD A PLAY SPACE FROM ROLLS OF NEWSPAPER TUBES TAPED TOGETHER INTO A WALL, A BRIDGE, OR A STRUCTURE LARGE ENOUGH FOR A CHILD TO ENTER.

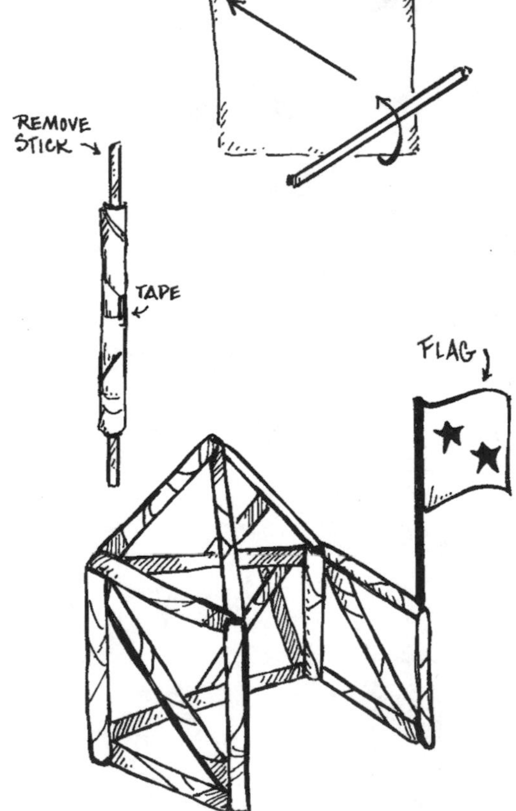

Materials

old newspapers
masking tape
stick or dowel
yarn, paper scraps, stickers, optional

Steps

- Roll newspaper around a stick or dowel to form a tube. Start by placing the stick diagonally across the corner of the newspaper as shown in the illustration. Roll up. Tape the loose end in the center. Then slide the stick out.
- Make many many tubes. Several hundred would create an amazing space!
- Tape the tubes together and build a play space. Use masking tape freely to make the building strong. Experiment making a:

cabin	cage
car	cave
hide-out	horse
jail	rocket
train	truck

- Enjoy this imaginary place space.

Streamer Zone

TRANSFORM AN ORDINARY ROOM INTO A MYSTERIOUS AND COLORFUL PLAY ZONE WITH STREAMERS ATTACHED TO A HULA HOOP.

Materials

rolls of crepe paper in any colors
lots of tape, a stapler, or pushpins
hula hoop
scissors
fan, optional

Steps

- Tape one end of a roll of crepe paper to a hula hoop. Cut the crepe paper at a desired length, perhaps 10′ (4 m) or more. Snip with scissors.
- Attach additional long strips of crepe paper, until the hoop is filled with strips of crepe paper.
- Place the hula hoop in the middle of the room on the floor. Pull one streamer out from the hoop and tape the end to the ceiling, a wall, or a piece of furniture. Do this with each streamer from the hoop. The streamers will drape all over the room, like a sunburst from the hoop in the center.
- Or, turn on a fan and blow the streamers gently with moving air.

NOTE: ADULT SUPERVISION NEEDED FOR THIS STEP.

- Play and pretend in this imaginative and colorful streamer space.

More Ideas

Suspend the hula hoop from the ceiling so that it hangs horizontally and the streamers make a canopy or umbrella of colors.
Hang streamers over windows or doorways.
Hang streamers straight down from the ceiling.

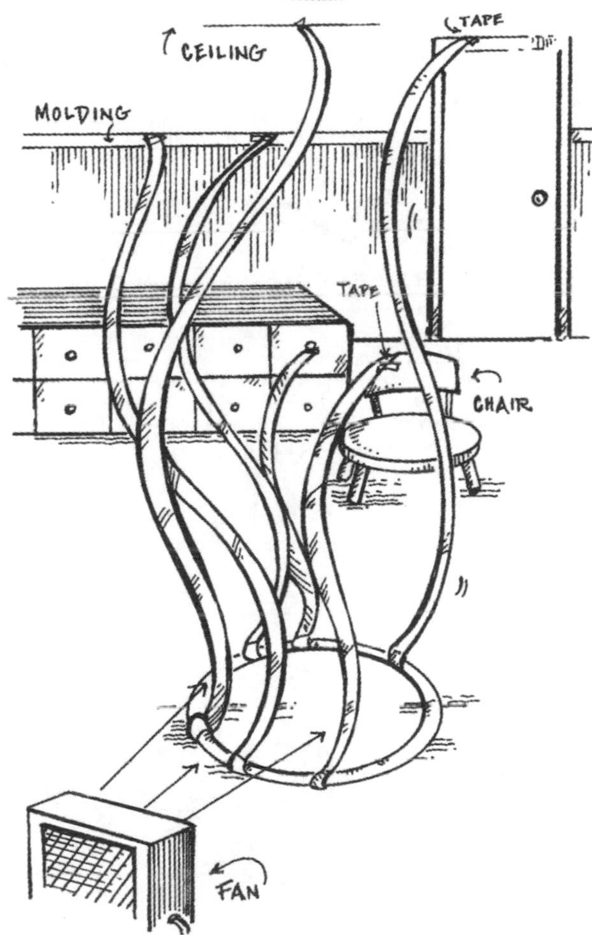

1 GLUE

Bag Block Building

Soft blocks constructed from used grocery bags stuffed with newspaper make for an easy building block experience. Knock them down—then build them up again!

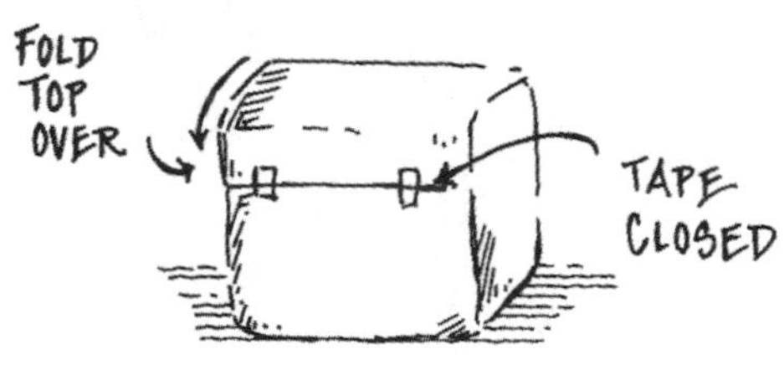

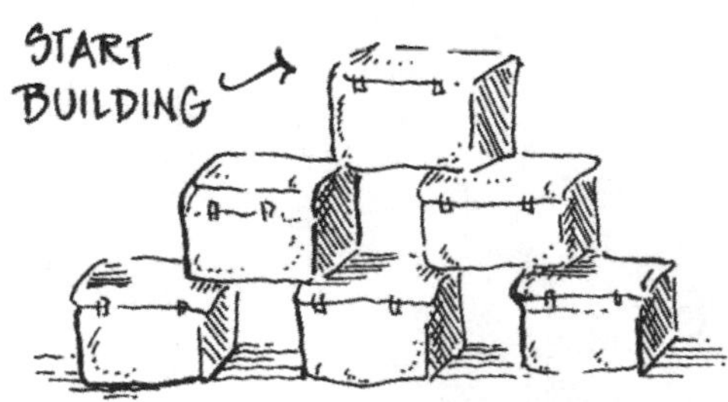

Materials

large paper grocery bags
old newspapers or any old paper
masking tape or packing tape

Steps

- Open a grocery bag. Stuff it with 10-12 double sheets of crumpled newspaper.
- Fold the bag opening over and tape the top closed. There is no need to decorate the bag unless you want to.
- Make at least ten or more blocks. Having 50 or more makes this activity most imaginative!
- Build a play space or other imaginary area.
- Blocks are soft and can be easily knocked down and built up again.

More Ideas

Supplement Bag Block Building with cardboard boxes, shoe boxes, or sheets of heavy paper for ramps, bridges, and roofs.

Make blocks from different-sized bags for smaller or larger blocks.

Room Weaving

1

Weave a crazy web of yarn or string throughout an entire room to create a wild and crazy play space.

Materials

string, yarn, ribbon, or twine
scissors

Steps

- Tie any smaller pieces of string and yarn together to make one long strand. Roll into a ball.
- To begin the Room Weaving, tie one end of the string or yarn to a doorknob, closet rod, bedpost, or chair leg.
- Take the string from one object to another, tying or wrapping around furniture or objects to hold it in place. String can crisscross itself and go all around the room like a web.
- Now weave and tie strings in between the first strings. A plan is not necessary, just keep tying and weaving strings to strings.
- When the web is done, imagine and play in the Room Weaving.

TIE SMALLER PIECES OF STRING and YARN TOGETHER
ROLL INTO A BALL

More Ideas

Pretend the Room Weaving is
  an imaginary world
  a spider web
  a thick jungle
  an underground cave
Add other materials, such as
  blankets or sheets • paper cutouts • strips of fabric • strips of newspaper

Obstacle Maze

Build a room full of obstacles and challenges for climbing, crawling, and hiding.

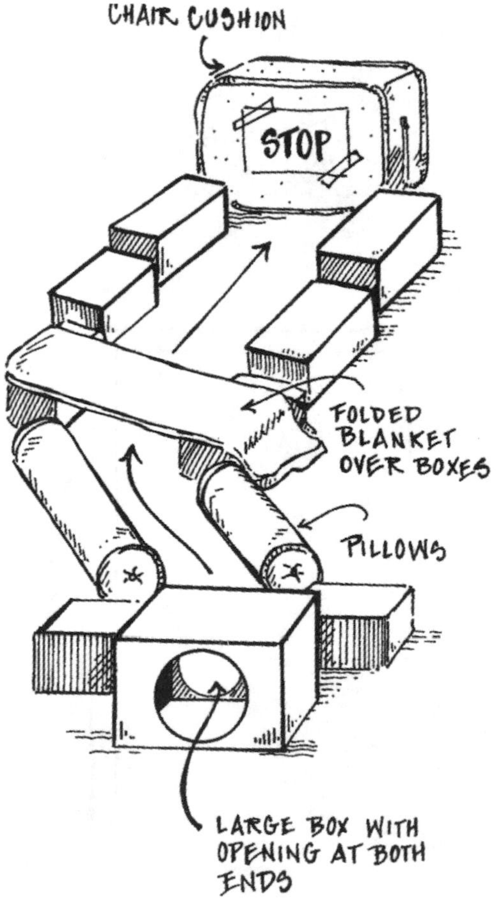

Materials

obstacle suggestions
- baskets • blankets • blocks
- cardboard boxes and cartons, all sizes
- chairs • cushions • other furniture
- pillows • tables • toys

Steps

- Set up obstacles and spaces for climbing, crawling, and hiding in a room or outdoor area. Begin with just a few obstacles.
- Suggestions:
    - drape blankets over chairs
    - create paths with blocks or boxes
    - stack pillows to roll over
    - turn tables on their sides like walls
    - pull couch cushions free to make a padded floor area or walls
- Play in the spaces.
- For an extra challenge, set up a specific obstacle course, such as
    - first, climb under table
    - then, roll over three pillows
    - then, jump over a line of blocks
    - then, wiggle through a gauntlet of chairs
    - finish with a jump into a pile of cushions

CHAIR CUSHION
STOP
FOLDED BLANKET OVER BOXES
PILLOWS
LARGE BOX WITH OPENING AT BOTH ENDS

Footprints Everywhere!

1

MAKE STICK-ON FOOTPRINTS TO CREATE A PATH OVER OBSTACLES, AROUND THE ROOM, OR EVEN OUTDOORS.

Materials

pair of shoes
marker
scissors
colored contact paper
carpeted floor

Steps

- Trace a pair of shoes on colored contact paper. Make as many pairs as desired—the more the merrier.

NOTE: IF ONLY CLEAR CONTACT PAPER IS AVAILABLE, TRACE FOOTPRINTS ON COLORED PAPER, CUT THEM OUT, AND COVER WITH CLEAR CONTACT PAPER RECTANGLES THAT ARE LARGER THAN THE FOOTPRINTS.

- Cut out the footprint pairs.
- Stick the footprints in a trail across the carpet or anywhere to make a path to follow. Footprints can go up and down ramps, stairs, through climbing toys, on rubber tire swings, outdoors, and everywhere!

NOTE: BE CAUTIOUS WHEN SELECTING SURFACES THAT MAY BE DAMAGED IF THE FOOTPRINTS ARE LEFT FOR EXTENDED PERIODS OF TIME.

More Ideas

Think of other kinds of prints to make, like handprints, paw prints, outer space appendage prints, or baby footprints.

Include alternatives to walking on the prints, like hopping on one foot or jumping on two feet.

Cardboard Carton Play

CONSTRUCT A HOUSE, CASTLE, CAVE, IGLOO, LONGHOUSE, OR FORT WITH A LARGE APPLIANCE BOX. JOIN SEVERAL BOXES TOGETHER TO MAKE CONNECTING ROOMS.

Materials

large cardboard box, such as from appliances or office furniture
knife to cut cardboard (adult only)
marker to draw cutting lines
duct tape, optional

Steps

- Work in an open, comfortable space inside or outside. Place the appliance box on the ground. Draw lines for windows, doors, chimney, or other features.
- Cut the cardboard with a sharp knife (adult only).
- Push the windows and doors so they will open and close easily. Use duct tape tabs for handles or openers on doors and windows.
- Add signs or additional features with the marker as needed.
- Other items and objects can be incorporated in the play, such as
  books • flashlight • paper and crayons • pillows • sleeping bag • toys of all kinds
- Time to play and pretend!

More Ideas

Design settings for specialized play, such as
for a cave—set up a play campfire
for an igloo—set up a play dog sled or ice fishing
for a castle—set up a play bridge and moat at the entrance
for a fort—set up a play horse corral
for the "Three Little Pigs"—make three houses side by side
for "Hansel and Gretel"—cover the house with candy designs
for a store—stock the shelves with inventory of choice

My Own TV

! ✂ 2 ★

CREATE A TELEVISION SET FROM A STRONG CARDBOARD APPLIANCE BOX, CRAWL INSIDE, AND PRETEND TO BE ON TV.

Materials

appliance cardboard box, strong and large (big enough to crawl inside)
felt pen or dark crayon
sharp knife (adult only)
stickers or labels, optional
masking tape or duct tape

Steps

- Draw a TV screen on one side of the box. Draw it as large as possible.
- Draw additional TV parts such as knobs, buttons, speakers. Stickers or labels can also be used for this step.
- Cut out the hole for the screen with the knife (adult only).
- Fold the flaps out on bottom of the box. Tape the box flaps to the floor to help keep the box from wiggling and collapsing.
- Crawl into the box and pretend to be on television.

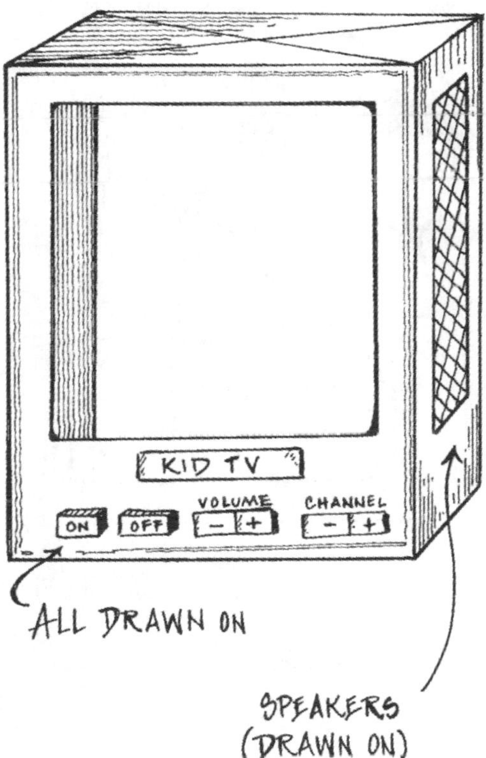

More Ideas

Make up a commercial. Hold an empty cereal box, toy, or other prop to sell.
Sing a song or act out a favorite book or story.
Ask a friend to change the "channel" for a new "program."
Use an old cabinet-style TV set with all the parts removed.

2 Art Gallery, Just for Me!

Creativity soars when inspired by these art frame and display ideas.

Materials

cardboard
chalkboard
drawing pad
magnetic board
marker board
old picture frames
shelf
table top
windowsill
decorating and frame making supplies, such as
crayons • fabrics • felt squares • glue • magnets • markers • paints and brushes
pencils • picture hangers • scarves • stapler • tape
children's artwork
paper scraps, stick on labels, and pens for making labels and signs

Steps

- Set aside a wall for the gallery showing area. Include the tops of tables and shelves or a windowsill for display.
- Decorate old picture frames, cardboard, or other display items with paint, markers, or other materials.
- Next, hang the empty picture frames, chalkboard, cardboard, magnetic board, or other display items in the gallery area. The purpose is to have display areas that the artist can reach independently to show off artwork. For example:
  slip a drawing behind an empty picture frame and attach with tape
  attach an artwork to a magnetic board with magnets
  display a sculpture on a felt square on the windowsill
  arrange artworks on a bookshelf draped with a scarf

Note: With beginning artists, use only one type of display. More experienced artists will appreciate more framing choices.

- Make signs and labels with paper scraps to name the artworks and list the artists' names.
- Invite friends and family to gallery showings.

Plastic Jug Structure

ASSEMBLE PLASTIC GALLON JUGS TO BUILD AN IGLOO-LIKE DOMED STRUCTURE. START SAVING JUGS AHEAD OF TIME BECAUSE ABOUT 200 ARE NEEDED FOR A FULL-SIZE STRUCTURE!

Materials

200 plastic gallon jugs, from water, juice, or milk (clean and dry)
NOTE: ASK FRIENDS AND FAMILY TO SAVE JUGS!
hot-glue gun (adult only)

Steps

- Place 20 jugs, bottoms facing out, in a circle on the floor.
- Remove four or five jugs in one spot to create a doorway.
- Connect the remaining jugs in the circle to each other with a hot-glue gun (adults only).
- Glue a row of jugs, moved slightly in toward the inside of the circle, on top of the first row. The number of jugs for each consecutive row will decrease from the original 20. This will begin the formation of the dome shape.
- Continue adding rows of jugs, moving them slightly in, until the structure is five rows high and the door is formed. A domed igloo-like shape should be forming.
- When gluing the sixth row of jugs, continue connecting jugs in a full complete circle. This will create a row of jugs over the door and begin the formation of the roof.
- Add rows of jugs until you have room at the top of the structure for only one last jug.
- Play and imagine inside the structure.

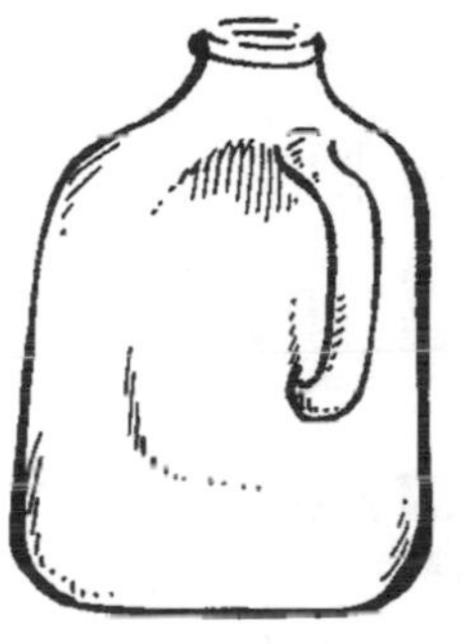

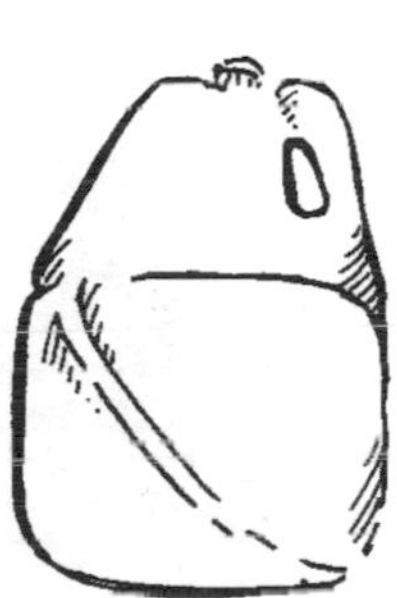

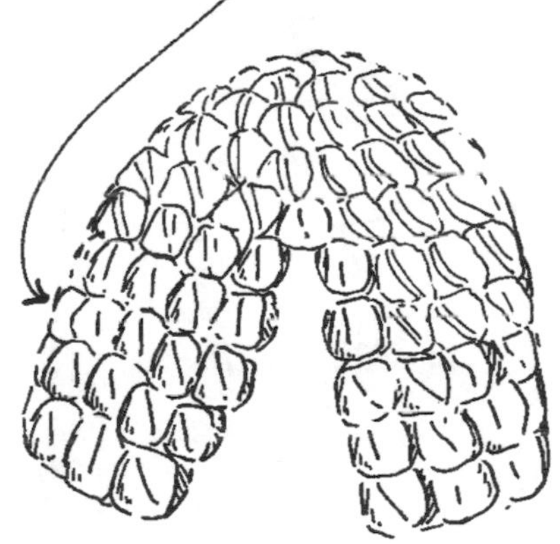

More Ideas

Use duct tape instead of a hot-glue gun.
Build a structure that is square or another shape.
Build a structure with shoeboxes or other boxes instead of jugs.
Build a structure with liter bottles or other plastic bottles instead of jugs.
Create an "Arctic World" with ice-fishing outside an igloo, toy polar bears and seals, a dog-sled, and other props.

Two Pretend Planetariums

IMAGINE BEING A PART OF THE NIGHT SKY, FLOATING IN SPACE OR TRAVELING TO ANOTHER PLANET. CREATE A STAR-GAZER'S DREAM PLANETARIUM AND A BIG DIPPER PROJECTOR.

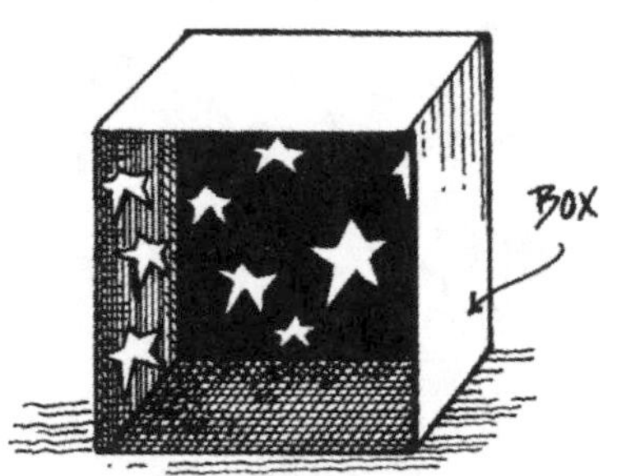

SPRAY PAINTED BLACK INSIDE
STICK ON STARS

Materials

large cardboard appliance box
black spray paint (adult only)
tape
glow in the dark stick-on stars (or cut-out foil stars)
flashlight
heavy paper cup, like a paper coffee cup
pen
poking tool, like a pointed pencil
dark room

Steps

Star-Gazer's Dream Planetarium

- Spray paint the inside of the appliance box with the black spray paint (adult only). Let dry completely.
- Turn the box on its side so the box can be entered from one end. Tape the other end closed.
- Place stick-on glow-in-the-dark stars on the inside black walls of the box. Make real or imaginary constellations.
- Star-gazers climb inside with a flashlight and explore the night sky.

Big Dipper Projector

- Draw seven dots on the bottom of the large, heavy paper cup in the design of the Big Dipper. (See illustration.)

NOTE: OTHER CONSTELLATION PATTERNS, REAL OR IMAGINERY, CAN BE MADE AFTER TRYING THE BASIC BIG DIPPER CUP IDEA.

- With adult help, poke seven holes through the seven dots.
- Turn off the lights and shine a flashlight through the cup.
- Project the Big Dipper onto the ceiling or wall.

Paper Off-the-Wall Scenery

CHANGE A BLANK WALL INTO IMAGINATIVE SCENERY FOR PRETEND AND PLAY.

Materials

large sheets of craft paper, different colors (available on tear-off rolls from school supply stores)
scissors
masking tape or pushpins
colored paper, crayons, stickers
other props for imaginative play

Steps

- Decide what scene to depict, such as a neighborhood, under the sea, outer space, western ranch, fairy glen, and so on. Imagine what this scene might be like, then choose the appropriate colors of craft paper. A neighborhood scene will be described for this example.
- Design the main background. For example, for the neighborhood scene, the large paper can be cut to look like a house, grass or lawn, a sidewalk, blue sky, trees, and windows. Draw and cut out the paper. Attach each paper to the wall with masking tape or pushpins.
- Add details to the neighborhood scene with other colored paper, crayons, or stickers. For example, make shutters for the window, a door knob, a bird in a tree, apples in the tree, a cat on the roof, flowers in the grass, and so on. Imagine the scene the way you would like it to be and start decorating and creating!
- Now that the wall is transformed into a neighborhood scene, play in the new scene. Bring in other props to make the play more imaginative. Some possibilities might be a wagon, tricycle, baby carriage, doll, or toy lawn mower.

NOTE: IF THE SCENERY WILL BE LEFT UP FOR AN EXTENDED PERIOD OF TIME, REMEMBER THAT AFTER SEVERAL DAYS THE MASKING TAPE MAY PEEL THE PAINT AWAY WHEN REMOVED.

2 Painted Off-the-Wall Scenery

Transform one wall in a room into an imaginative, permanent play space.

Materials

wall paint and brushes
masking tape
pencil
painters' paper, an old sheet, or newspaper
chalkboard paint and brush
cork sheet (from a roll) and glue, optional
materials suitable to the scene of choice, such as
screw hooks • Velcro • clothesline • fencing

Steps

- This more permanent version of transforming a play space requires more planning than the Paper Off-the-Wall Scene (page 29). A Neighborhood Scene will again be described for this example.
- Purchase paints, brushes, and other supplies from a home improvement store or lumberyard. The room should be emptied and well-ventilated before beginning. Protect carpeting or flooring with painters' paper, an old sheet, or newspaper.
- With a pencil and masking tape, design the scenery on the wall. For the neighborhood scene, create a central house design, and then add green lawn, blue sky, and possibly some trees or other details. Use the chalkboard paint for the green lawn. Paint the scenery and allow time for drying.
- If desired, glue cork sheeting to the wall for the trunks of the trees or a fence.
- Let everything dry.
- Brainstorm ideas for other things that might be fun to add. Paint details as desired, such as a bird in the tree, doorknob, flowers in the yard, and so on. Dry.
- Set up toys and furniture to encourage play. Draw with chalk on the green lawn and use pushpins on the cork boards.

More Ideas

Add three-dimensional ideas such as
attach a real door knob or nail on a small fence
attach a real mailbox to the wall
use Velcro to attach lightweight objects to the wall like puppets or toys

Fingerpainted Ocean

2

CREATE AN UNDERSEA WORLD, DISPLAY FISH AND CRAB CREATIONS IN THE MURAL, THEN PRETEND AND PLAY BENEATH THE SEA.

Materials

big display wall with empty floor space nearby
large craft or butcher paper
tempera paint
liquid starch
pushpins, tape, stapler, glue
blue cellophane, optional
paper and paper scraps
pens, crayons, paint, and brushes
scissors
art tools for "finger" painting, such as
  forks • kitchen utensils • rubber gloves • scraps of wood • sponges • variety of paintbrushes
props, optional
  beach blanket • crown • fishing pole • sand and sand toys • rocks and shells
  swim-flippers • sunken model ship • treasure chest

Steps

- Spread a huge sheet of paper out on the floor. The paper should be large enough to cover the wall.
- Pour puddles of liquid starch on the paper. Sprinkle dry or pour liquid tempera paint into the puddles of starch. For authentic looking ocean, the colors painted at the top of the mural should be lighter, and those deeper in the ocean should be progressively darker.
- Fingerpaint and use other tools to swirl and create designs in the ocean. Fingernails, the edges of spatulas or rulers, combs, forks, rubber gloves, and other utensils add texture and design to the Fingerpainted Ocean. Let dry.
- Cover the dry painting with blue cellophane, if desired. The cellophane gives the painting a three-dimensional look.
- Hang the ocean mural on the wall at child height, with the lower edge touching the floor if possible. Or suspend a wire from one corner of the room to the other with eye hooks, then staple the mural to this wire. Use the suspended wire for other hanging projects throughout the year.
- Create cut-out sea-life, such as crabs, octopus, sand dollars, starfish, fish, sharks, and whales. Attach these to the ocean painting.
- Place props (see above) near the mural to complete the imaginative space, or play in the ocean area as is.

Little Scenes & Mini-Play

Chapter 2

Little Pebble Family Home
Playdough Car and Track
Sandbox Town
Lost Garden Mini-Scene
Fantasy Tornado Bottles
Card Building
Shoebox Raceway
Real Mouse Maze
Meet Miss Aluma Crumple
Treasure Display Case
Realistic Bird Nest
Little Shoe Houses
Scrolling Story Box
Schoolie Spoolies
Berry Busy Zoo
Volcano Island Pool
Tropical Rain Forest Mini-Scene
Coral Reef Mini-Scene
Photo-Doll

1 !

Little Pebble Family Home

CREATE A FAMILY OF CHARACTERS FROM PAINTED PEBBLES OR SMOOTH STONES. THE PEBBLE FAMILY STORES NICELY IN A SHOEBOX DECORATED AS A ONE-ROOM HOME.

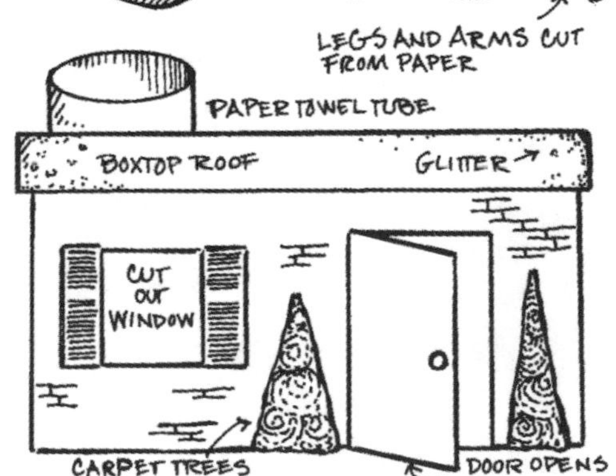

Materials

oval pebbles or smooth stones
newspaper
acrylic paint and brushes
decorating materials for people or houses, such as
 aluminum foil • cardboard • carpet scraps • cotton balls • craft eyes • flooring scraps
 glitter glue • markers • paper scraps • permanent markers • plastic wrap
 sewing trim • sticky dots • wallpaper scraps • yarn
scissors
glue, tape
shoebox or any strong box
knife to cut box (adult only)

Steps

- Spread out the stones on newspaper.
- Paint the rocks like a family, with the biggest stones being the parents, the smaller stones children, and the tiniest stone the baby. Let dry.
- When dry, the Pebble Family can be played with as is or decorated further. Glue on other decorative features like yarn hair, cotton beard, googly eyes, sticky dot cheeks, and glittery clothes. Dry again.
- Build the Pebble Family a house from any box on hand. Cut the windows and doors where the artist so designates (adult only). To decorate, think up ideas for making a nice, cozy home for the Pebble Family. Here are some suggestions:
    - Cover the windows with plastic wrap taped in place.
    - Glue scraps of fabric to the windows for curtains.
    - Slip in carpet or flooring scraps.
    - Build furniture from cardboard, tape, and glue.
    - Cover the walls with wallpaper.
- With the new house placed on a table or floor, invite the Pebble Family to move in and start enjoying their new home and all the adventures you can imagine! Who will they meet and what will they do? Is there a Pebble Family pet?

Playdough Car and Track

1 ★

Build a course with turns and challenges for toy cars for imaginative, pretend races and fun.

Materials

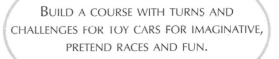

playdough (use recipe below, any other homemade recipe, or commercial play clay)
table (cover with newspaper or vinyl tablecloth)
toy cars

Steps

- Roll playdough into long thin sausages or snakes.
- Arrange them on the table, connecting them to make walls.
- Create matching walls about 3″ (8 cm) from the first wall. The track for the cars is in between these walls.
- Drive toy cars through the tracks, or roll playdough balls through the tracks.

More Ideas

Draw lines on butcher paper. Cover the lines with rolls of playdough snakes. Drive the cars between the rolls.

Build the tracks on a larger sheet of plywood or a board. Place the playdough board on an incline and roll the cars through the tracks.

Simple and Good Playdough Recipe

REQUIRES STOVE-TOP COOKING

- In a saucepan, mix 1 cup (240 grams) flour, 1 cup (240 ml) water, ½ cup (120 ml) salt, 2 teaspoons cream of tartar, and 2 tablespoons oil. Add food coloring if desired. Cook until thickened over low heat, stirring with a wooden spoon. Turn out on a bread board. Cool slightly and then knead. This recipe can be doubled or tripled as necessary. Store in a covered container to keep moist and pliable.

Sandbox Town

BUILD A TOWN WITH ROADS, TREES, HOUSES, PARKS, STORES, AND SCHOOLS IN A SANDBOX.

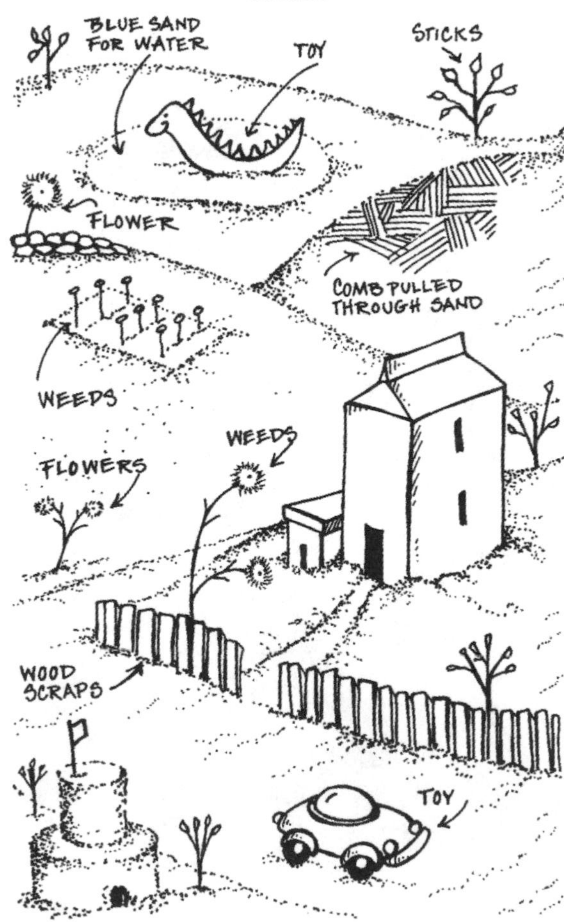

Materials

sandbox or sand table
water
building and shaping tools, such as
comb • flat piece of wood • soup can • spatula • spoon • tuna can
items to enhance pretend play, such as
blocks • cardboard • flowers and weeds • milk cartons • rocks • sticks and branches
toy cars • toy figures • wood scraps
colored sand, optional (Color plain sand by adding Liquid Watercolors or dry tempera powder to dry sand. Dry on newspaper.)

Steps

- Moisten sand with water so it will hold shapes like roads and hills.
- Work in the sand with a few of the tools suggested above to build a town with roads, playground, residential area, and town center.
- Add blocks or milk cartons for buildings. Add sticks and branches for play trees. Add rocks, toy cars, and figures.
- Play with the village.
- Consider coloring some sand and using it to decorate as needed. For example, green sand could represent lawns or parks, brown sand little gardens, black sand the roads, and so on.
- When play is over, mix the sand together again and return it to regular use in the sandbox. Toys, blocks, milk cartons, and other building supplies can be cleaned and reused or recycled.

More Ideas

Think of a theme to design and build, such as
another planet • dinosaur land • farm and barnyard
picture perfect flower garden • zoo

Lost Garden Mini-Scene

Create a miniature garden in a baking pan with real plants, dirt, and rocks. Add a little toy figure or two to play in the garden.

Materials

baking pan
soil and sand
collected plants, weeds, flowers, branches, and sticks
pebbles or gravel
materials for a "pond," such as
  aluminum foil • dish of real water • hand mirror
optional materials for building garden accessories, such as
  craft sticks for a fence • Lincoln Logs for a small cabin • toothpicks and glue for building garden furniture
toy figurines or mini-action figures of choice to play in the garden, such as
  action figure • animal • car • dog or cat • elf • horse • person • statuette
water in a spray bottle

Steps

- Fill a baking pan (or other large container) with soil. Pat firmly. Build up one end of the pan as a hill or incline, if desired.
- Put real plants into the soil. Pat dirt around plants firmly.
- Sticks and small branches pushed into the dirt look like trees. These will last for some time with moist soil.
- Build sand pathways lined with pebbles.
- Partially bury a reflective piece of foil or a small mirror in the soil to look like a pond. A dish of water will resemble a pond too.
- Add other ideas, like a Lincoln Log cabin or a fence made of craft sticks. Glue toothpicks together to make a bench or other garden furniture.
- Play in the garden with a toy person or animal figure.
- Keep the garden moist with water from a spray bottle.

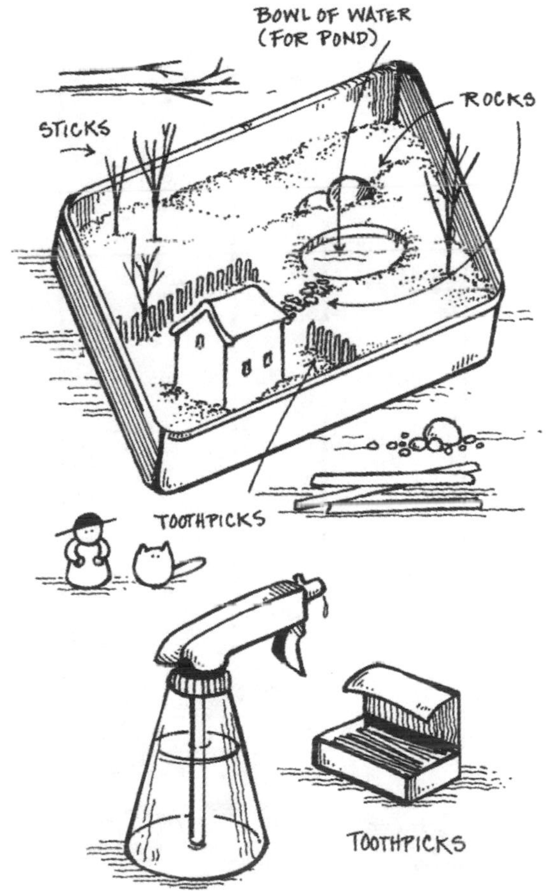

More Ideas

Construct a larger garden or scene in a sand table, sandbox, or washtub.

1 Fantasy Tornado Bottles

CREATE FANTASY TORNADOES FROM ALL KINDS OF AMAZING MATERIALS. HOW BEAUTIFUL AND MYSTERIOUS THEY LOOK AS THEY SWIRL IN THEIR CONTAINERS!

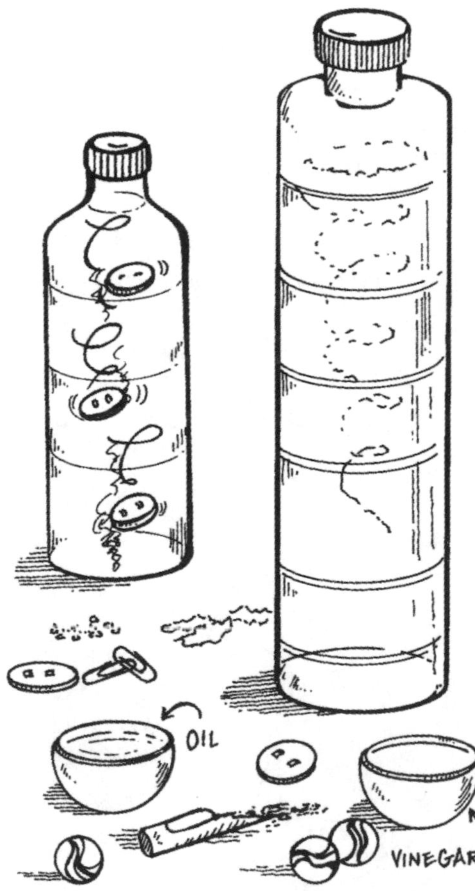

Materials

several clear plastic water bottles (one for each tornado), with tight-fitting lids
liquids to fill the bottles, such as
colored water • metallic Liquid Watercolors • oil • shampoo • vinegar • water
materials to add to the bottles, such as
bits of foil • buttons • chopped Easter grass • colored paper clips
glitter, sequins • marbles • metallic confetti • pieces of corks
sand • shaved crayons • shredded cellophane

Steps

- Partially fill bottles with any of these liquids:
  - clear shampoo
  - half water, half oil
  - Liquid Watercolor, metallic variety
  - shampoo and oil
  - water
  - water, oil, vinegar
- Then add floating, swirling materials from the materials list. Try just one or a combination. Some favorite combinations to experiment with are:
  - gold Liquid Watercolor paint (about 1 oz.) with water
  - half-colored water, half oil
  - long crayon shavings in water
  - oil with marbles
  - shampoo with oil
  - water with glitter and sequins
  - water with paper clips
- Screw on the cap nice and tight. Swirl to create fantastic tornadoes.

Card Building

BUILD
A ONE-STORY HOUSE OF CARDS WITH AS MANY ROOMS AS POSSIBLE. DON'T FORGET THE ROOF! IF A BIG TORNADO COMES ALONG AND BLOWS IT DOWN, BUILD IT UP ALL OVER AGAIN!

Materials

one or more decks of cards, or sturdy cards cut from poster board or old file folders
carpeted floor
patience

Steps

- Balance two cards against each other (see illustration) in a T shape forming two walls of a card house.
- Lean a third card against the first two to form the third wall.
- Add more cards and walls to the first room. Make the building as big as you like. Leave door openings into the rooms.
- Gently add a roof of cards.

NOTE: BE PREPARED FOR THE HOUSE OF CARDS TO COME TUMBLING DOWN!

More Ideas

Add little toys or dolls to live and work in the card building.
Pretend to be a tornado and blow the houses down, then build them all over again.

Shoebox Raceway

Visit a shoe store and volunteer to recycle their throw-away empty shoeboxes into a cardboard raceway for toy cars, trucks, and other wheeled vehicles.

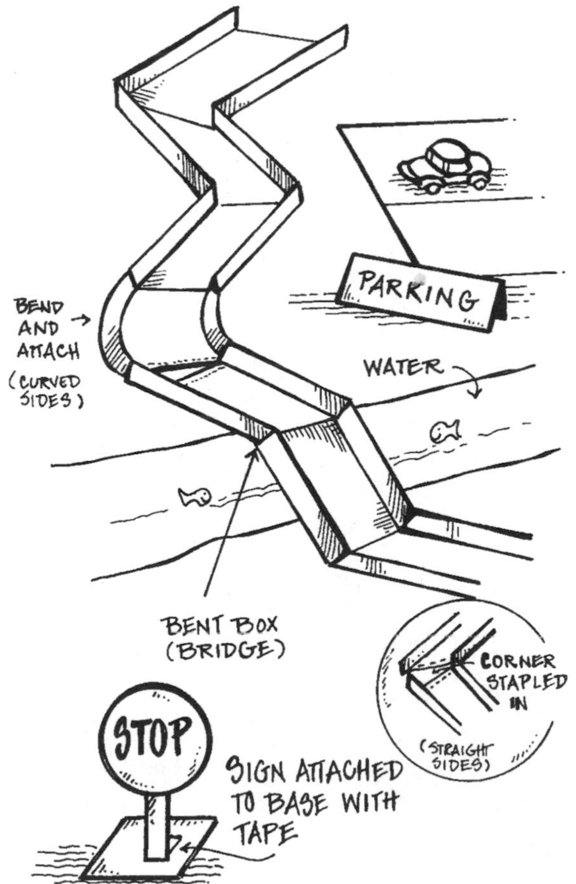

Materials

variety of shoeboxes and lids, cereal boxes, tea boxes
scissors
tape, stapler, glue
old file folders
cardboard and paper scraps
markers

Steps

- Collect all types of lightweight cardboard boxes, especially lids of shoeboxes.
- Cut away the two short ends of the lids to make sections of walled track (see illustration).
- Join the lids with tape.
- To form curves, cut strips of lightweight cardboard, and staple (see illustration).
- With additional boxes, cardboard and paper, build bridges, overpasses, gas stations, and taxi stands.
- Draw parking spaces on a large sheet of cardboard. Use this as a parking lot for the vehicles. Add arrows and directional signs for traffic control.
- Bring in the vehicles for raceway and traffic play.

More Ideas

Construct traffic signs and signals from paper and cardboard scraps.
Build an entire town with any of the following:

airport	raceway
bus depot	schools
farm	stores
houses	train station
marina	zoo
park	

Real Mouse Maze

! 2

LITTLE BITES OF FOOD AT THE END WILL ENCOURAGE THE MOUSE TO EXPLORE THESE PUZZLING TRAILS.

Materials

pet mouse (gerbil, hamster, rat, guinea pig, rabbit)
NOTE: ADULT SUPERVISION IS NEEDED TO ENSURE THE SAFETY OF THE PET.
wooden building blocks
open floor area to build maze

Steps

- Assemble the wooden blocks in an open floor area.
- Build a simple pathway for the mouse (or other pet) that has no openings for the mouse to escape. Keep in mind that sometimes they crawl over the block walls. Place a food reward like a seed at the end of the path.
- With adult supervision, place the mouse at one end of the path and see if the mouse crawls to the other end to find his reward. Hooray, the mouse did it! But that was just practice. Place the mouse back in his cage to rest, then build a more complicated maze experience.
- Build a maze of pathways with corners and turns. Some paths will end, and others will connect and keep on going. Decide where to place the food rewards.
- Again with adult supervision, place the mouse at one end of a pathway. Watch to see if the mouse can find the treats.

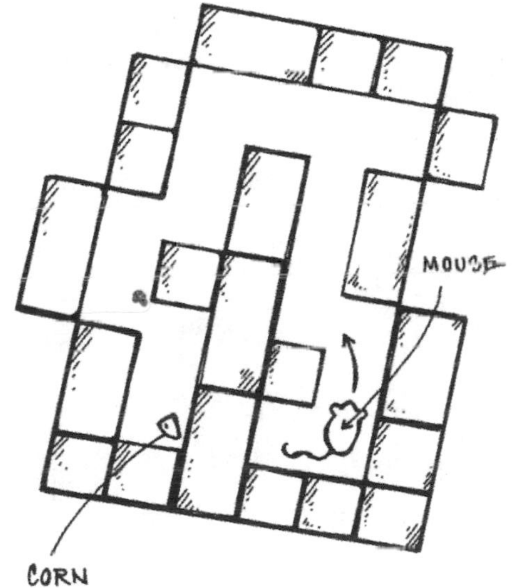

More Ideas

Keep a graph of which types of food rewards are favorites or are found quickly, and which are not.
Give the mouse nesting materials to build a little nest in part of the maze.
Let the maze lead into the mouse's regular cage and see if it will go into the cage or turn around and head back into the maze.
Read *Mouse Paint* by Ellen Walsh, *Seven Blind Mice* by Ed Young, and other mouse books.

1

Meet Miss Aluma Crumple

CRUMPLE AND SHAPE SHEETS OF ALUMINUM FOIL INTO BODY FORMS OF PEOPLE, PETS, AND FAMILY MEMBERS, READY FOR POSING AND PLAYING INDOORS AND OUT.

Materials

aluminum foil
scissors
tape or stapler, optional

Steps

- Tear a sheet of aluminum foil from the roll (about 12″ x 15″ or 30 cm x 40 cm). Heavy duty or regular foil both work well.

NOTE: THE STRONGEST AND EASIEST PEOPLE AND PETS TO POSE ARE MADE FROM ONE PIECE OF FOIL, RATHER THAN JOINING SEVERAL PIECES.

- Mold and squeeze the rectangle into the shape of a person. Tear the foil to separate for legs and arms, keeping the foil in one piece in the center (see illustration). This may take some experimenting and exploring. If necessary, use a stapler or tape to hold things together.
- Pinch and model other sheets of foil into more characters and pets.
- Play with the figures.

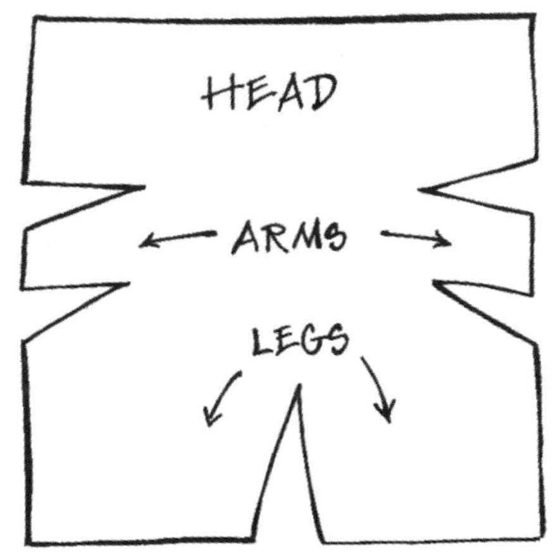

More Ideas

Create a house for the family from a big cardboard box.
Pose the family and take a photograph or draw a picture of them.
Put on a little show with the characters, telling an Aluma Crumple story.

Treasure Display Case

! GLUE 1

Display an enchanted crown, a golden egg, or Jack's magic beans in this imaginative display box.

Materials

something special to put on display, like a wishing rock, an enchanted crown, a golden egg, or even the magic beans for Jack in the Beanstalk
a lightweight hinged box, like those that tea bags or doughnuts come in
scissors
glue, tape
decorating materials, such as
clear plastic wrap, optional • crayons or markers • glitter • hobby jewels and gems
magazine pictures • paints and brushes • paper scraps • sequins • sewing trim in gold or silver • shiny ribbon • stickers • wrapping paper

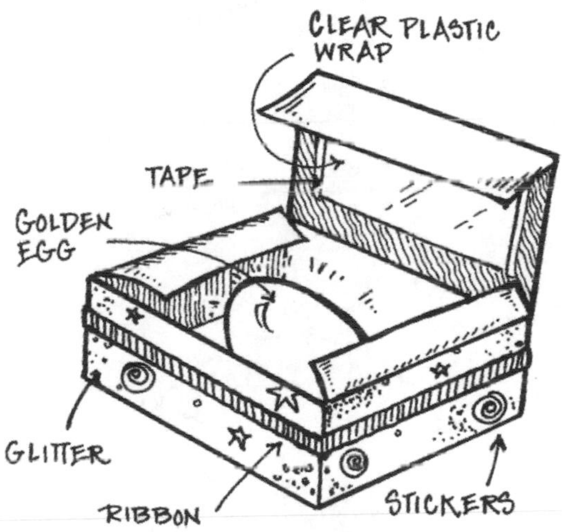

Steps

- Cut a see-through window in the lid of the hinged box. To do this, first poke a little hole with scissors to get started, and then finish cutting the window. Leave about a 1″ (3 cm) frame around the cut-out window so it will be strong.
- Next decide how to decorate the box. If you decide to paint it first, let the paint dry before gluing on anything else.
- Decorate the box with glitter, sequins, bits of colored paper, ribbons, or stickers.
- If desired, pull a piece of clear plastic wrap from a roll. Stretch it across the inside of the window and tape it in place.
- Now the box is ready to display your magical object. Place it inside the display box, close the magical door, and peer inside to see the enchanted object waiting for imagining to begin.

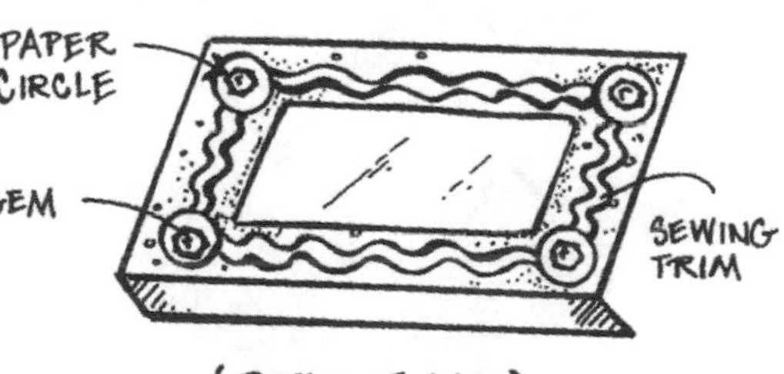

More Ideas

Read a special story or fairy tale, then make something special to go in the display box from that story, like the poison apple from "Snow White" or a bowl of porridge from "Goldilocks and the Three Bears."

Realistic Bird Nest

CONSTRUCT AN AUTHENTIC-LOOKING BIRD NEST BY HAND FROM MUD, GRASS, AND TWIGS. COMPLETE THE SCULPTURE WITH A "NUT BIRD" AND COLORFUL EGGS.

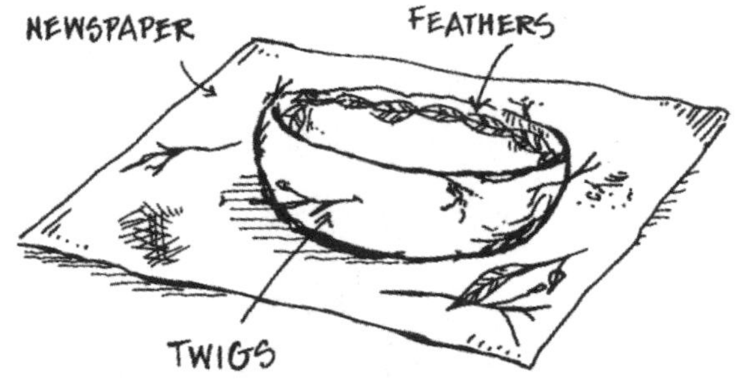

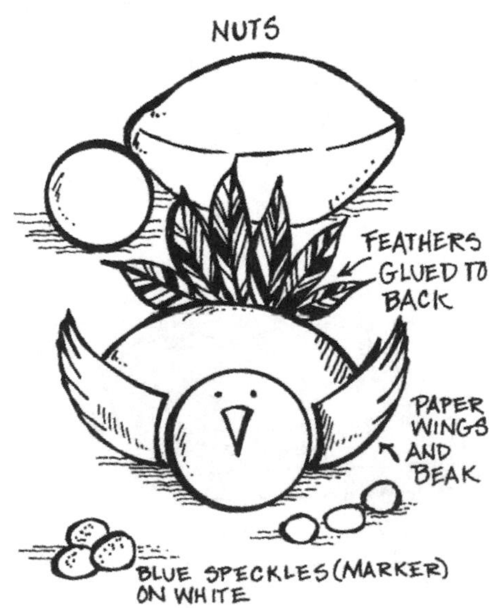

Materials

newspaper
dirt (2 to 3 cups) (480–720 ml)
water
twigs
grasses
bowl
walnut (or pine cone)
hazelnuts
glue
black permanent marker
paper scrap for the beak
feathers, craft or collected natural
white tempera paint
paintbrush
colored markers
scissors

Steps

The Nest

- Scoop the clean dirt into a bowl. Mix with water until the consistency of thick clay.
- Mix in some grasses and twigs. Squeeze and mix, forming a nest shape. Line the nest with feathers, if desired. Place the nest on the newspaper to dry over night.

The Bird

- Glue a hazel nut (or other round nut) for the head on a walnut or pine cone (or other larger nut) for the body with white glue. Hold until the nuts start to adhere to each other. Or use a glue-gun (adults only) as a fast-drying alternative. Let dry overnight.
- When dry, draw eyes on the head of the bird with the permanent marker.
- Glue on a little diamond shape of paper to look like a beak. Paper wing shapes or feathers could also be added to the body, if desired (see illustration).

The Eggs

- Paint several round nuts completely white. Let dry overnight.
- Decorate the nuts with colored markers to look like fancy bird's eggs. Swirls, spots, and other designs are effective.
- Place the little bird and eggs in the nest and display it anywhere. Or for fun, place it in a houseplant or protected tree.

Little Shoe Houses

After creating shoe houses from an old pair of shoes, make some little wood scrap people to live in them.

Materials

newspaper
old pairs of shoes, adult sizes work well (For a village of shoe houses, collect sneakers, high heels, sandals, boots, nurse's shoes, and so on.)
collection of decorating supplies and craft items, such as
beads • brushes • buttons • coffee stir sticks • fabric scraps • felt
glitter glue • markers • paints • paper • ribbon • sewing trims
straws • wallpaper • wrapping paper •yarn
glue, tape, staplers, safety pins
wood scraps in small cylinder or block shapes
paint and brushes, markers, crayons

Steps

- Spread out some newspaper on the work space with all the craft materials assembled.
- Decorate the shoes to resemble little houses.
- Make blocks of wood into people to live in the shoes. Draw or paint on their features. Stick on fabric pieces for clothes. Yarn is good for hair. Remember the Old Woman who lived in a shoe? She had so many children she didn't know what to do!

More Ideas

Build a shoe village on a sheet of cardboard or large paper with roads, sidewalks, gardens, and playgrounds drawn with markers or made with scraps of paper glued on the cardboard.
Build a swing set, school, or store from cardboard boxes, straws, and other collected materials.

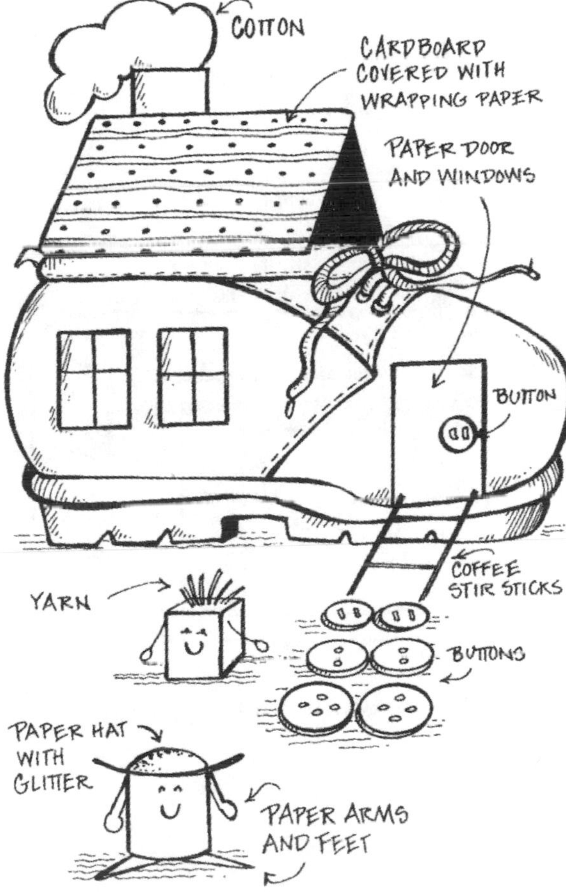

Scrolling Story Box

MAKING UP A STORY THAT MOVES ACROSS A VIEWING SCREEN IS A GREAT IMAGINATION BOOSTER FOR ALL AGES. TRY AN ORIGINAL STORY OR ONE BASED ON A FAVORITE BOOK, FAIRY TALE, SONG, OR MOVIE.

Materials

cardboard box, strong and medium sized
tape
scissors (or sharp knife for adult only)
crayons, markers
long roll of butcher paper (or sheets of paper taped together to make a long roll)
2 wooden dowels about 12″ (30 cm) long (or an old broomstick or paper towel tubes)

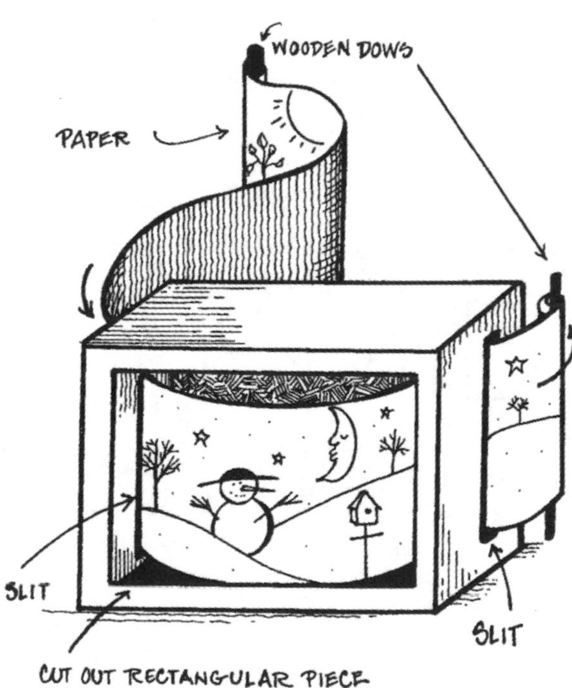

Steps

- Cut a rectangular piece from the smooth side of a cardboard box for the viewing screen. Next cut two slits in the side ends of the box a little bigger than the paper width, about 12″ x 2″ (30 cm x 5 cm) (see illustration).

NOTE: AN ADULT SHOULD ASSIST WITH THE CUTTING STEPS, OR IF USING A KNIFE, SHOULD DO ALL OF THE CUTTING.

- Spread the roll of paper out on a table or smooth floor space with the beginning edge at the right, and any extra paper to the left.
- Think of a story, book, fairy tale, song, or movie to draw. Draw the story on the roll of paper in a sequence of events, from the first thing that happens to the last thing that happens. When finished drawing the story, reroll the paper onto a dowel or paper towel tube with the right edge (where the first picture is) free.
- To prepare the drawings as a show, feed the paper from the left slit and across the viewing rectangle to the right slit. Pull it through and tape it to the second dowel or paper towel tube. Now the drawings are ready to scroll.
- Slowly roll the drawings from the left to the right onto the dowel. Tell the story out loud, or simply enjoy viewing the drawings.
- When finished, roll the drawings back onto the left dowel or paper towel tube.

More Ideas

Add music or a story tape to enhance the show.
The first "page" in the viewing window could be a title, design box, or sign.

Schoolie Spoolies

GLUE 2

MAKE CLASSMATES FROM EMPTY SPOOLS OF THREAD, SITTING AT THEIR PAPER CUP TABLES AND DESKS. SAVE ONE BIG SPOOL TO MAKE INTO A HELPFUL TEACHER.

Materials

school box (cigar box)
scissors
empty thread spools (3 or more)
glue and tape
scraps for decorating, such as
fabric scraps • paper scraps • rubber bands • sewing trim • stickers
paper cups
permanent markers
pipe cleaners for arms and legs, optional
construction paper or other paper

Steps

- Open a school box or cigar box as shown in the illustration. This will be the school. Cover the inside of the box with construction paper, or leave plain.
- Decorate the school room with scraps to show a window, walls, bulletin board, and floor. Add any other embellishments as desired.
- To make the classmates, wrap a pipe cleaner around an empty spool and twist to resemble arms. Pipe cleaner legs can be inserted into the base of the spools or omitted. Decorate the spools with paper or yarn hair. Draw faces with permanent pens. Add paper or fabric scrap clothing. Construct a teacher from a large spool.
- Construct desks, tables, and chairs from paper cups. Cut them to fit the spools. Turn the cups over for desks, or leave them up for chairs. The spools can sit in the cups.
- Create and construct any other details for the room, such as
  carpet • library • painting • toys
- Arrange the room for learning time. Play and pretend with the spoolies.

More Ideas

Using the cigar box as the basic form, think of other ideas to construct, such as
gas station • library • restaurant • toy store • zoo
Build bigger scenes for play with larger cardboard boxes.
Select several boxes and join them together to make a school with more rooms.
Build a town with many different places for the spoolies to shop, play, learn, and enjoy themselves.

Berry Busy Zoo

PLASTIC BERRY BASKETS MAKE REALISTIC PLAY CAGES FOR MINI-ZOO CLAY ANIMALS. REMEMBER TO LEAVE THE GATES UNLOCKED SO THE ANIMALS CAN FROLIC ON THE BUTCHER PAPER ZOO GROUNDS.

Materials

play clay recipes (see next page)
large sheet of butcher paper or craft paper (open sheets of newspaper are a good substitute)
paints and brushes, optional
toothpicks

berry baskets	tape
labels, blank	cardboard
markers	scissors
paper	small boxes, milk cartons, containers

Steps

- Model zoo animals of any kind from the cornstarch clay (Funclay). Dry overnight until hard. Paint if desired, then dry again. Suggestions for zoo animals are
  alligator • baboon • bear • bison • chimpanzee • elephant
  giraffe • gorilla • kangaroo •lion • seal • tiger
- Spread the butcher paper out on the floor or a table. Think about zoos, real or imaginary. Begin to plan the layout of the cages and the zoo grounds. Think about including one or more of the following:
  monkey island • penguin pools • seal pools
- Draw pathways connecting the areas where the cages will go. Draw the places for other areas like pools, shops, playground, or grazing fields.
- Place the berry baskets on the zoo design for cages. Make doors by cutting open a wall of the basket with scissors so doors will open and close. Add flags, if desired, with plain labels sandwiched over toothpicks and attached to the cages. Labels also make great stick-on signs.
- Place the animals in the cages.
- Make other buildings or things for the zoo from cardboard, scrap paper, boxes, containers, tape, and glue.
- Play and pretend in the Berry Busy Zoo.

Three Sculpting Dough Recipes

ALL OF THESE RECIPES CAN BE DOUBLED OR TRIPLED

Basic Breadcraft

EXCELLENT FLOUR AND SALT DOUGH

- Combine 4 cups (1 L) flour and 1 cup (240 ml) salt in a bowl.
- Make a well in the center and pour in 1 cup (240 ml) water. Mix with hands. Add up to ½ cup (120 ml) more water and continue mixing by hand. Dough should form a ball but not be crumbly or sticky.
- Knead five minutes on a floured board until smooth. If desired, knead in tempera paint or food coloring for color.
- Work with small portions of dough on foil or wax paper.
- Bake (with adult help or supervision) zoo animals for one hour at 325°F until hard. Then cool. Can be painted when cool.

Funclay

SMOOTH WHITE DOUGH, DRIES IN SEVERAL HOURS

- Mix 2 cups (480 ml) salt and ⅔ cup (160 ml) water in a pan.
- Mix 1 cup (240 ml) cornstarch and ⅓ cup (80 ml) cold water in a bowl.
- Bring the pan of salt and water to a boil (adult help or supervision needed). Then mix in the cornstarch and water.
- Knead on wax paper until dough-like. Knead in tempera paint or food coloring, if desired.
- Now sculpt and model with the clay. Remember to pull clay out to make arms, heads, and legs rather than sticking separate pieces on.
- Dries in several hours. Can be painted when dry.

Basic Play Clay

WHITE AND HARD, DRIES QUICKLY

- Mix 1 cup (240 ml) baking soda with ½ cup (120 ml) cornstarch in a pan.
- Add about ⅔ (160 ml) cup water and stir until smooth.
- Cook over medium heat. Boil until like mashed potatoes (adult help or supervision needed).
- Pour on a board to cool. Then knead. Add color to the dough with drops of food coloring or paint, if desired.
- Sculpt and model the clay. Let dry for an hour or so.
- For a protective coating, paint with nail polish or any clear hobby coating.

Volcano Island Pool

CREATE AN IMAGINARY TROPICAL POOL IN A CHILD'S WADING POOL, FILLED WITH HANDMADE FISH, BOATS, AND A CENTRAL VOLCANIC ISLAND.

Materials

child's wading pool, filled halfway with water
scissors
permanent markers
materials for creating an island in the pool
  beach towel • black plastic • trash bag • twist tie
materials for creating boats that float, such as
  aluminum foil • bubble wrap • heavy paper • milk cartons
  plastic containers • wood scraps
materials for creating shrink-art tropical fish
  aluminum foil • clear salad bar containers • hole punch
oven set to 275°F (140°C)
paper clips or washers
permanent markers
spatula and cookie sheet
yarn
other toys to add to the island pool, optional

Steps

- Set up the pool on the grass outdoors or in a suitable play area. Fill halfway with water.
- To construct a play tropical island, place a beach towel in the plastic garbage bag. Seal the garbage bag with a twist tie. To resemble a volcanic island, place the bag upside down in the center of the pool, with a pointed corner of the bag sticking up. (If the bag starts to float, open the bag again and soak the towel in water to weigh it down. Reseal and place in the center of the pool.) Shape the bag a little to look like a volcano. If the bag continues to float, add a brick or rock inside the bag as extra weight.
- Construct floating boats from wood scraps, shapes formed from aluminum foil, or other materials that will float. Decorate boats with flags or other items if desired.
- To create the tropical fish, draw directly on clear plastic from a salad bar container with permanent markers. Plastic will shrink about 50%, so plan ahead. Cut the fish out. Place them on a foil-covered cookie sheet in the 275°F (140°C) oven until shrinking is complete (adult help or supervision needed). This will take only a few moments. Remove from the oven and press flat with a spatula. Punch a hole in each fish and tie with a piece of yarn.
- Attach paper clips to the yarn strands to act as weights so the fish will sink under the surface of the water. Sometimes several clips are needed for heavier fish. Place the fish in the pool.

Tropical Rain Forest Mini-Scene

! GLUE 2

Build a mini-rain forest, then add characters and animals to the scene. The scenery panel begins with a cardboard box opened up into a three-part panel.

Materials

good-sized cardboard box
glue, tape, stapler
paints, especially green
papers such as
  art tissue • construction paper • corrugated paper • crepe paper
scraps such as
  felt scraps • nylon stocking • packing peanuts • sewing trim
aluminum foil or paper foil to resemble a river
hot glue-gun (adult only), optional
scissors, paintbrushes
sand or salt

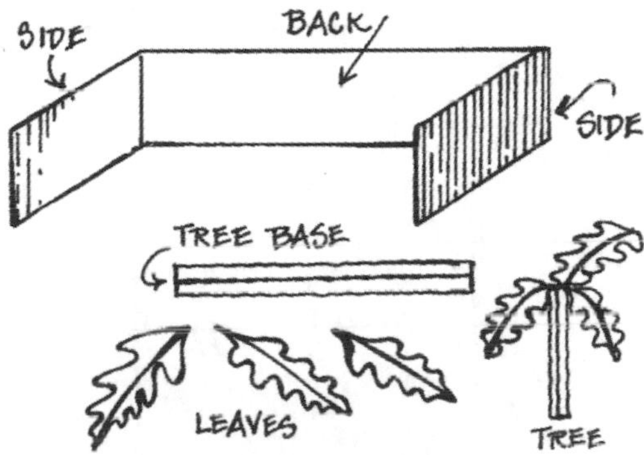

Steps

- With adult help, cut away the bottom, top, and one side of the box. Save for use in another project or recycle. The remaining three-sided panel will be the base for the scenery. Place it on the table and help it stand up to view.
- Now place the scenery panel flat on the table. Decide what to put in the rain forest, including such things as
  birds • blossoms • fruit • insects • monkeys • river • snakes • trees • vines
- Cut out strips of corrugated cardboard for the trees and glue them on the panel.
- Further cut and glue other vegetation and fruits, leaves, and blossoms with the bright art tissue or construction paper. Cut and glue animals, birds, insects, and monkeys typical to a tropical rain forest.
- Glue a long strip of aluminum foil or a bright foiled paper to resemble a river or pond.
- Sand or salt can be glued on to look like sand or ground.
- Stand the scene up on the floor to dry. Meanwhile, find some toys to bring to the scene. Snakes and monkeys or other stuffed toys would work well.
- Play beside the tropical rain forest scenery, imagining and pretending.

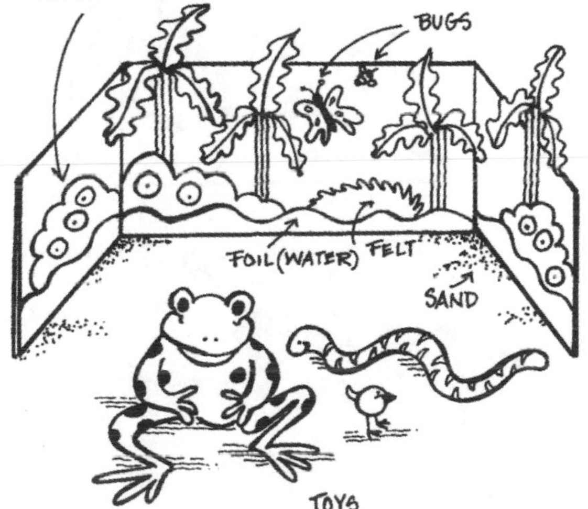

More Ideas

Use the basic three-panel form to create scenery for any imaginative play. Some suggestions are:
  airport • circus time • fairy glen • firefighters • insect playground • outer space • pet hotel

Coral Reef Mini-Scene

TURN AN EMPTY BOX INTO A MINI-SCENE REPRESENTING A CORAL REEF COMPLETE WITH A WIDE VARIETY OF TROPICAL SEA LIFE FROM SEA TURTLES TO JELLYFISH AND ANGEL FISH TO BEAUTIFUL CORAL.

Materials

good-sized shallow cardboard box
glue, tape, stapler
tempera paints and liquid starch
scissors
paintbrushes and mixing cups
thread
papers such as
  art tissue • construction paper • drawing paper
tools to etch designs in paint, such as
  comb • fingernails • markers or crayons
paper clip
hot glue-gun (adult only), optional

Steps

- Turn the box on its side like a theater. Cut away the flaps facing the audience. The bottom of the box will be the back of the scene.
- To paint the background of the coral reef, mix blue tempera paint and liquid starch in one cup and green tempera with liquid starch in another cup. With paintbrushes or fingers, paint the insides of the box with swirls and waves of blue and green paint to resemble the colors under the sea. Dry.
- To make seaweed, mix other colors of paint in addition to the blue and green such as yellow and orange with liquid starch. Dip a small sponge into any of the paints. Dab here and there on a sheet of white paper. Dab different colors all over the paper until it is filled in. Drag a comb, paper clip, or fingernails through the paint to etch designs in the wet paint. Then dry.
- Cut the paper as shown in the illustration in any design to resemble seaweed. By leaving a fold at the bottom, the seaweed can be glued to stand up in the scene. Glue the seaweed into the box.
- Crumple up balls of brightly colored tissue paper to resemble coral. Glue this in between the seaweed.

- Look in books to see what kinds of tropical fish live in a coral reef. Draw, paint, or color many different kinds of fish. Color both sides of the fish, if you like. Cut them out. Cut pieces of thread, tape each fish to a thread, and tape each thread to the top of the scene so fish will look like they are swimming in the seaweed above the coral.
- Design other sea life to add into the scene like shellfish and jellyfish.
- Read about life on a coral reef. Then imagine scuba diving in the undersea world of the coral reef.

More Ideas

Apply the basic form of a theater-style mini-scene box for other ideas, such as
baby nursery • busy city • dense jungle • farm yard • secret garden • starry galaxy

Drop several drops of different colors of paint onto a 5″ x 7″ (13 cm x 18 cm) piece of Plexiglas. Place another piece of the same size on top of the drops of paint and gently press down. Remove the top piece of Plexiglas and press onto a piece of paper over and over. Do the same with the bottom piece of Plexiglas. The prints look just like underwater coral. Just add seaweed and water, fish and starfish!

Photo-Doll

CONSTRUCT A STAND-UP PAPERDOLL FROM A PHOTO OF A REAL PERSON, CUT AND GLUED TO FOAM-CORE BOARD.

Materials

camera and film (adult only)
foam-core board
bathing suit
rectangular wood scraps
(about 2″ x ½″ or 5 cm x 2 cm)
photographs
paper
scissors
drawing tools (crayons, markers, pencils)
white glue
x-acto knife (adult only)

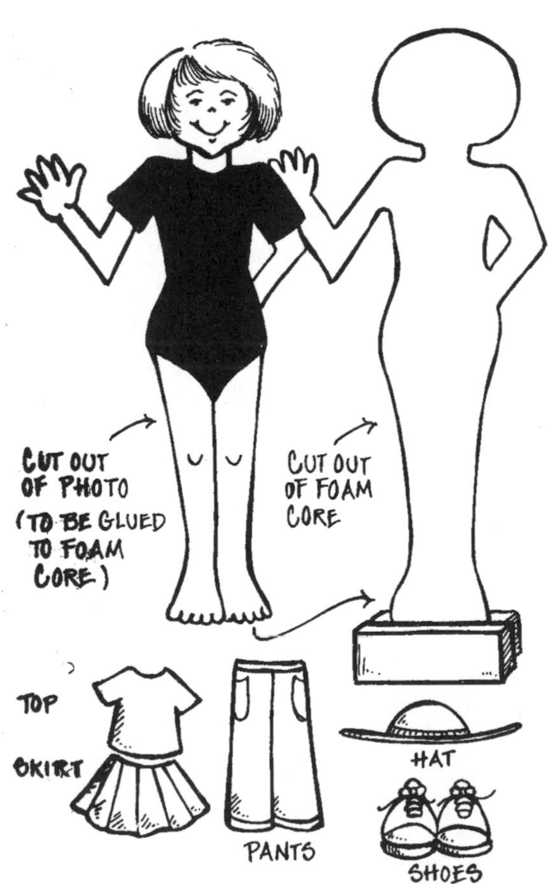

Steps

The Paperdoll

- Prepare to be a paper doll model! Dress in a bathing suit like real paper dolls. Stand in good light against a plain wall in a pose that will work well for clothing, such as facing directly forward with one hand on a hip and the other hand waving. Try several poses.
- An adult takes a picture of the paperdoll model. Suggestion: Turn the camera to get a nice, tall shot of the entire body. Be sure to take shots of several different poses that will work well for different clothing.

NOTE: INSTEAD OF TAKING PHOTOS, SIMPLY PHOTOCOPY ANY EXISTING FULL BODY PHOTO OF A CHILD, ENLARGING TO A GOOD-SIZED PAPER DOLL SHAPE.

- Have the film developed, but request 5″ x 7″ (13 cm x 17 cm) enlargements (or photocopy and enlarge smaller poses). Select a favorite pose. Carefully cut out the selected photo of the paper doll model.
- Trace the basic shape of the photo on the foam core with a pencil. Cut through the foam core with an x-acto knife along the outline of the body (adult only). This will be the basic paper doll.
- Glue the photo to the basic foam-core shape, spreading the glue thin and smooth so the photo won't wrinkle. Dry.
- To stand the paper doll, sandwich two little scraps of wood to the base of the paper doll with glue. Hold briefly until set. Then finish drying (overnight works well).

The Clothing

- When the doll is dry, photocopy it on a copy machine. Cut out the body shape. This will be the body pattern for making clothing to fit.
- With a tiny piece of tape, stick the pattern to a window with good light coming in. Then hold a sheet of plain white paper over the pattern. Draw the beginnings of clothing like a simple shirt and pair of pants. Remove the paper from the window to a table and finish adding all the details. Color it with crayons, markers, or colored pencils. Then cut it out.
- To dress the doll, stick a small loop of tape on the back of the outfit and press it to the doll to hold.
- Make more outfits and play dress-up with the paper doll.

Puppets and Sets

Chapter 3

1 Easiest Stick Puppet

THESE ARE THE EASIEST PUPPETS IN THE WORLD TO MAKE AND ARE FUN TO USE.

Materials

heavy paper
crayons or markers
scissors
yarn
googly craft eyes
popsicle sticks, craft sticks, or tongue depressors
tape or glue (staplers work too)

Steps

Idea One

- Draw a face on the end of a craft stick or tongue depressor.
- Glue on a little yarn hair or googly eyes, and the puppet is ready to go.
- Try gluing a paper costume to the stick.

Idea Two

- Draw a puppet shape such as a person, animal, or object on the heavy paper. Color it in.
- Cut it out and tape or glue the puppet to a popsicle stick.
- Help the puppet dance, sing, or act.

More Ideas

Design the puppet in two layers, with a front and back. Draw and color the back of the puppet too. Glue the two pieces together with the stick in between.

Make all the characters from a favorite story or song.

Construct a simple puppet stage from a cardboard box.

Pointer Puppets

1

Materials

markers or make-up pencils
fingers

Create only one index finger puppet or draw up to five or ten! Toes and bare feet are fun to decorate too.

Steps

- Draw a face on one finger pad with a marker or a make-up pencil.
- Want more than one puppet? Create faces on each finger. Give them different personalities and facial expressions such as those in the illustrations.
- Act out a story using one of these puppet stage ideas: crouch behind a table turned on its side or behind a couch, or hang a towel over a broomstick between two chairs. (See other puppet stage ideas on pages 70, 80, 82, 85 and 86 in this chapter.)

More Ideas

For costumes, tape a little rectangle of fabric or paper around the finger.
For hats, stick a little ball of clay on the fingertip. Mold and shape for different hat types.
For funny arms, loosely twist a pipe cleaner around the first knuckle so that two ends of the pipe cleaner are hanging free to look like arms.
A handful of Pointer Puppets make a great choir or band!

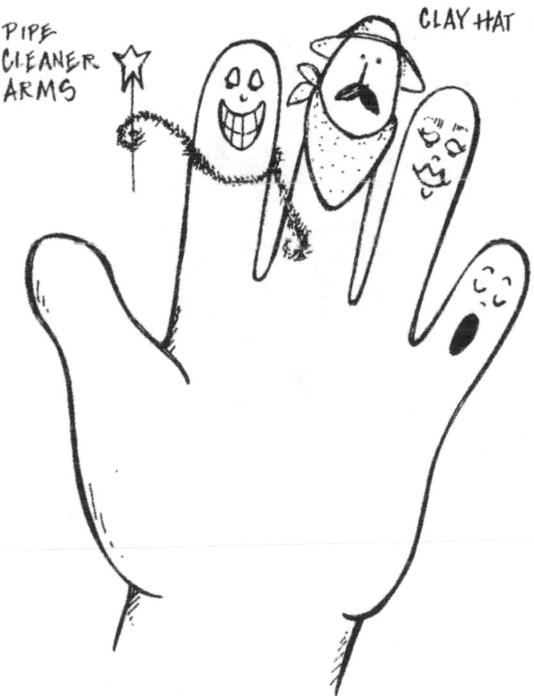

1 GLUE

Cup Puppet

MAKE A LIVELY PUPPET WITH ONLY A PAPER CUP, GLUE, AND A FEW DECORATIVE SCRAPS. THE CHILD'S HAND "WEARS" THE PUPPET AND MAKES IT COME TO LIFE!

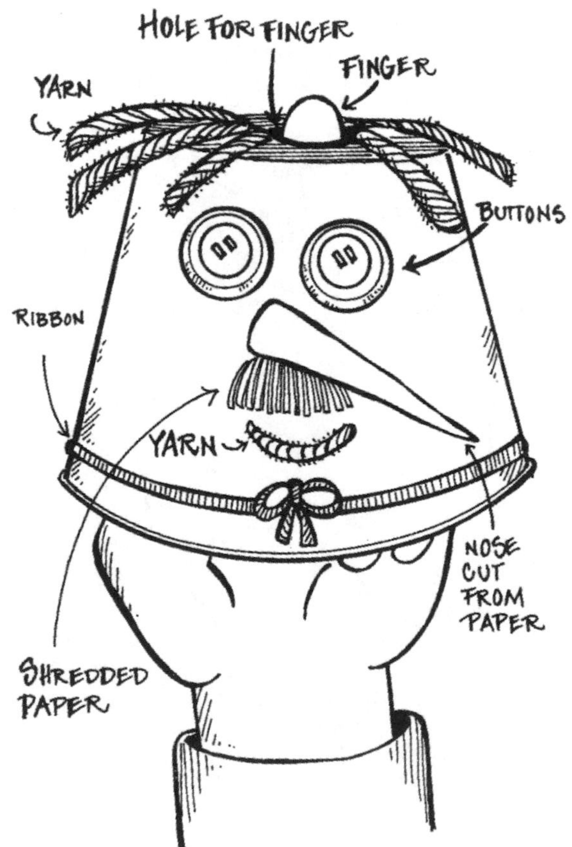

Materials

paper cup or Styrofoam cup
pencil or scissors to poke hole
glue
decorative materials, such as
buttons for eyes • collage items • googly craft eyes • paper scraps for clothes
sewing trim for decoration • shredded paper • wallpaper • yarn for hair
sleeve of old shirt with button cuff for costume, optional

Steps

- Poke a hole the size of a child's finger in the bottom of the cup.
- Turn the cup upside down on the workspace.
- Begin gluing decorations on the cup, creating a puppet head and hair with buttons, yarn, paper scraps, and other trims or scraps.
- Allow the puppet head to dry.
- To operate the puppet, the child pokes his pointer through the cup and out the hole just a bit. The hand will be mostly inside the cup.
- If desired, wear a cut-off button cuff sleeve for the cup puppet's clothes or costume.

Ballet Fingers

GLUE 1 ★

ACT OUT A STORY BY DANCING OR PUT ON SOME MUSIC AND DANCE "ON POINT" WITH THIS FINGER PUPPET.

Materials

pencil
poster board
markers
scissors
nail polish, any color
construction paper scraps
dancing fingers
glue
googly craft eyes, optional
materials to make a tutu, such as
fabric scraps • lace • paper doily • paper scraps • pipe cleaner • sewing trim • small bubble wrap

Steps

- Sketch the torso of a dancer's upper body with arms out or above the head, or any combination of arm positions. Some adult help may be required to make the body large enough. Use the base pattern provided here, if desired.
- Cut out the dancer's body.
- Glue on construction paper details such as a hairdo, leotard, or other dancing outfit.
- To create a tutu, gather some lace about 12″ to 18″ long (30 cm to 45 cm) or other scrap on a pipe cleaner and attach to the torso by twisting the pipe cleaner around the waist. Bubble wrap and doilies make pretty tutus too.
- Glue on googly craft eyes if desired or draw with markers.
- Cut two finger holes near the lower edge of the torso.
- Paint the nails of the two dancing fingers with nail polish to look like dancing slippers.
- Put on music for free dancing, or dance out a favorite story or fairy tale.

More ideas

Using this puppet idea as a basic form, create other characters, such as
angel • clown • gingerbread man • grandmother • monkey
police officer • robot • teacher

1 S'aw Right Puppet Hand

THIS HAND-PUPPET IDEA COMES BY WAY OF THE OLD ED SULLIVAN SHOW OF 1950'S TELEVISION FAME.

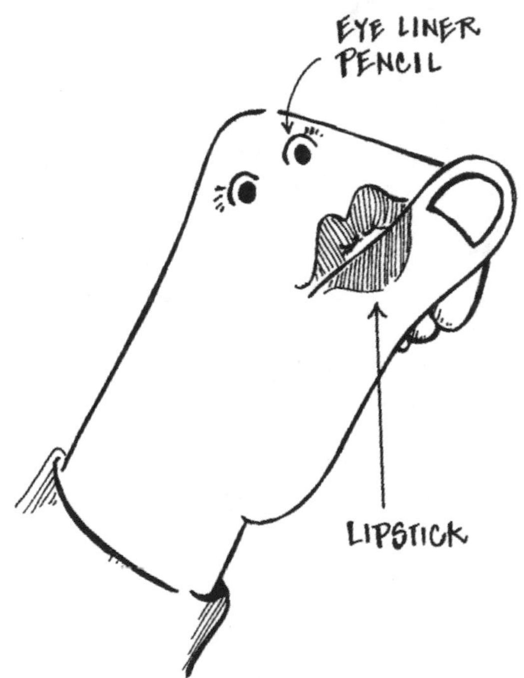

Materials

hand
lipstick or face paints
eyeliner pencil
optional materials for making hair, a hat, or a crown, such as
felt • glue • paper • scissors • tape • yarn

Steps

- See the illustration for the best way to hold the hand to create a moving, talking mouth shape. Practice moving and wiggling the thumb to create the mouth.
- Using lipstick or face paints, draw a mouth on the thumb and index finger. Paint on eyes above the mouth. Add eyelashes, eyebrows, or other smaller details with an eyeliner pencil.
- If desired, choose a decorative idea to finish the puppet, such as braiding yarn to make a little wig, cutting out a small crown or hat from paper, or using felt to make a hat.
- With a bit of tape or glue, stick the wig or hat to the knuckles of the hand puppet.
- The puppeteer on the Ed Sullivan show used to ask the puppet, "S'aw right?" And the hand puppet would always answer, "S'aw right!" By moving the thumb only for the puppet's mouth, while keeping it tucked into place, the decorated hand becomes a simple talking puppet. "S'aw right?" "S'aw right!"

Two Favorite Finger Puppets

THESE TWO PUPPET PROJECTS TRANSFORM ORDINARY FINGERS AND THUMBS INTO SOMETHING SPECIAL AND UNUSUAL!

Materials

plaster strips from pharmacy
(ask pharmacist for directions)
water
newspaper or paper towels
markers
saved lids from glue sticks
contact paper, optional
glue
scraps and collage materials, such as
cotton balls • googly craft eyes
sequins • yarn

GLUE STICK PUPPET

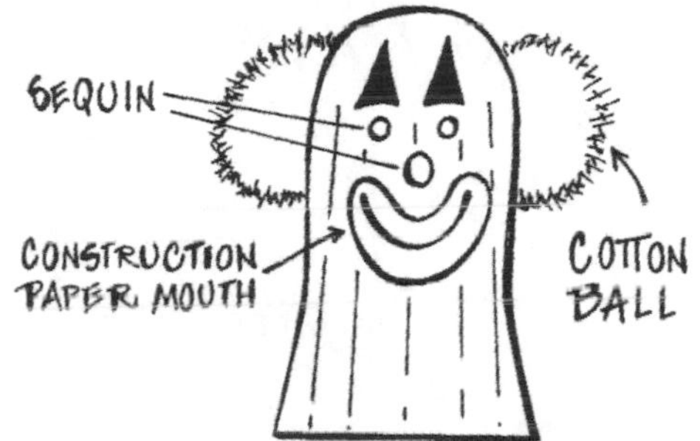

Steps

Plaster Thumb Puppet

- Dampen several plaster strips and wrap gently around the child's thumb.
- Smooth the wet plaster strips.
- Remove and let dry on newspaper. The thumb-shaped plaster will harden.
- When dry and hard, decorate with markers to make a finger puppet. Make as many puppets as desired.

Glue Stick Finger Puppet

- Cover glue stick lids with contact paper or use as is.
- Decorate with materials to create little puppets such as people, animals, babies, dogs, ghosts, or other imaginary characters. Experiment with materials for decorating the puppets. For example, yarn makes great hair, but so does a fluffy cotton ball glued on the top of the lid. Try different materials before gluing.
- When the glue is dry, enjoy as finger puppets.

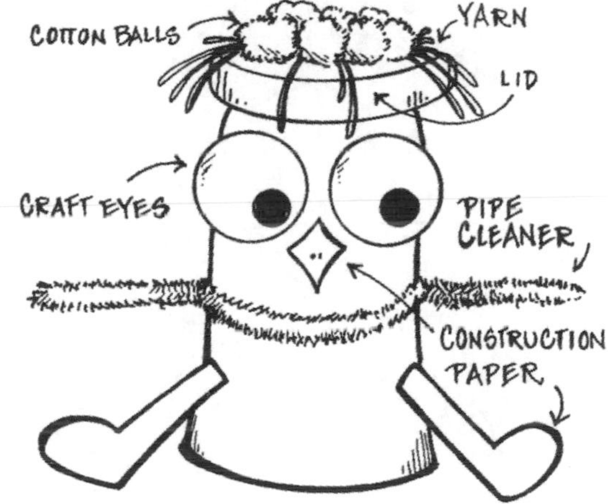

PLASTER THUMB PUPPET

More Ideas

To make a puppet theater out of a shoebox, cut away the bottom of the box and set the lid aside. Turn the box on its side and help the puppets perform inside the box. First decorate the box if desired. It's fun to come up with a sign for the theater or show too.

Finger puppets like dancing and singing best of all!

1

Paper Plate Puppet

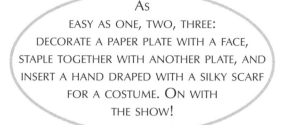

As easy as one, two, three: decorate a paper plate with a face, staple together with another plate, and insert a hand draped with a silky scarf for a costume. On with the show!

Materials

2 plain white paper plates
stapler
paper and yarn scraps
glue, tape
scissors
crayons or markers
scarf

Steps

- Staple two white paper plates together, insides facing each other. Leave a space open on one side for the hand to be inserted between the plates. Staple every inch or so all the way around so the puppet will hold together through performance after performance.

Note: For extra strength, tape the plates together over the staples.

- With paper scraps and drawing tools, design a puppet face on one side of the paper plate. Add other features such as yarn hair, cut-out glasses, beard, or hat.
- Drape a silky scarf over the hand the puppet will go on. Then slide this hand into the paper plate—like wearing a big round mitten.
- The puppet is complete, including a scarf costume! On with the show!

More Ideas

Happy-Sad Flip-Over Puppet: Create a happy face design on the back of one paper plate and a sad face on the second plate, then staple them together. The puppet can turn back and forth to show its emotions. Different voices can be used for each side of the puppet.

Other "Flip-Over Puppet" ideas:

asleep and awake
day and night
girl and boy
mean and nice
old and young
Red Riding Hood and Wolf
tortoise and hare

Finger Puppet Theater

GLUE 1 ★

Create a puppet theater out of a strong paper plate that finger puppets can use as an inventive, created-to-size scenery.

Materials

strong paper plate (such as Chinet)
scissors
construction paper scraps
glue
sticky dot or white label, optional
permanent marker

Steps

- Cut a slit in the middle portion of the strong paper plate.
- With scraps of construction paper, cut shapes and things to create a scene on the plate with trees, clouds, or any other ideas. Glue them on the plate.

Note: Items can cover the slit, but must be cut apart to keep the slit open.

- Take a permanent marker and draw a face on the pointer finger. A plain sticky dot or white label can be drawn on first and then stuck to the finger, if preferred.
- Hold the plate upright and insert fingers though the slit of the plate for an instant puppet theater.

More Ideas

Make puppets on popsicle sticks, tongue depressors, coffee stir sticks, or straws instead of fingers.
Create a scene from a story or book, and use the puppets to retell the story.
Use additional finger puppets with the plate theater.

1 Best Easy Puppet Stage

Two chairs, an old sheet, and a broom handle are all that is needed to construct this easy puppet theater.

Materials

2 straight-back chairs
broom handle
string, optional
old sheet

Steps

- Place two straight-back chairs back to back.
- Place the broom handle from one chair to the next.
- Pull the chairs apart until the broom handle is still hanging over the edges of the chairs with room to spare.

Note: Tie the broom handle to the chair backs for extra stability, if you like.

- Throw the sheet over the broom handle so it touches the floor on the front side, and hangs over on the back side.
- Crouch behind the sheet and put on a puppet show!

More Ideas

Decorate the sheet with paint, paper scraps, or pieces of fabric.

Instead of a broom handle, find three pieces of thin wood similar to a yardstick and each about the height of the chairs. With string, tie one stick straight up to the left chair, one to the right chair, and then one across to both of the chairs. Attach a curtain to the piece of wood across the chairs. Glue or pin scenery to the sticks for the puppet shows.

Old Glove Finger Puppets

GLUE 2 ★

An old glove is the perfect beginning for easy, effective finger puppets.

Materials

old glove
scissors
decorations to sew or glue on, such as
buttons • scraps • sequins • yarn
needle and thread or fabric glue

Steps

- Cut the fingers from an old glove.
- Decorate each cut-away finger with eyes, hair, mouth, beak, whiskers, nose, or whatever it needs. Make real or imaginary characters with different personalities.
- Wear one finger puppet or wear all five.

More Ideas

Decorate an entire glove or mitten as a puppet, without cutting it apart.

As with any puppet, make up a story to act out, or base a show on a favorite book, song, or story.

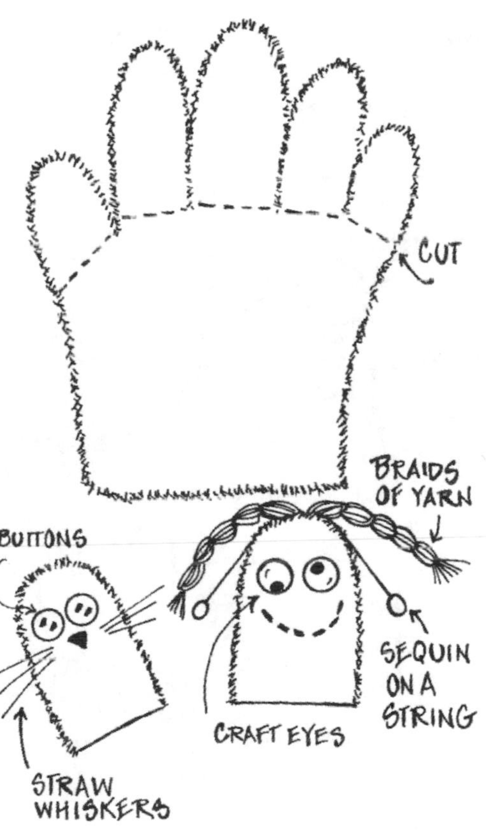

Wacky Rubber Glove Puppet

OLD RUBBER GLOVES COME IN BRIGHT COLORS, ARE BAGGY, AND INSPIRE THE CREATION OF WACKY RUBBERY CHARACTERS!

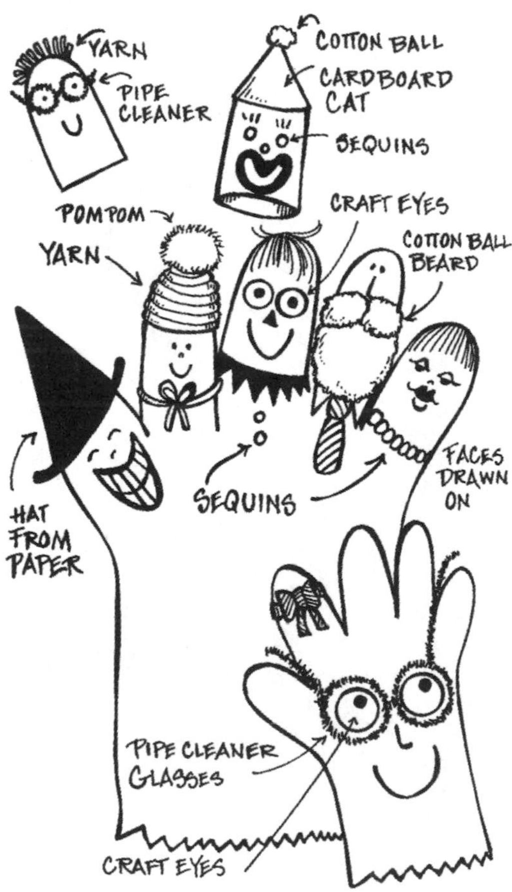

Materials

old rubber glove
scissors
scraps for decorating, such as
    paper scraps • plastic scraps • rubber glove scraps
choice of glue, such as
    cool glue-gun with adult supervision
    hobby adhesive for use on vinyl or plastic (look in craft stores)
    tacky glue
tape, stapler
decorative or collage materials for puppet features, such as
    buttons • googly craft eyes • permanent markers • pompoms • sequins • yarn

Steps

Finger Puppets

- Cut the fingers from an old pair of rubber gloves. Each finger will be one puppet.
- Decorate each rubbery tube with collage materials, or draw features on the tube with permanent markers. Consider making little hats, crazy hair, glasses, beards, tails, wings, or other imaginative features for each puppet. Or choose to create specific characters from a favorite story, like the three little pigs and the dreaded wolf.
- Slip the tubes over fingers and enjoy acting and performing, singing and dancing.

Full Hand Puppet

- Leave the entire old rubber glove intact. Do not cut finger tubes off.
- Decorate the puppet as a wacky rubbery character using collage materials and permanent markers as described above.
- If there is more than one rubber glove, make additional characters for an entire production or show.

Sock Puppet

SEW BUTTONS, BEADS, AND YARN OR FELT SCRAPS ON AN OLD SOCK TO CREATE A PUPPET CHARACTER. A "MUST-DO" PROJECT FOR ALL CREATIVE PUPPETEERS!

Materials

old sock
materials for decorating, such as
beads • buttons • felt scraps • fringes • googly craft eyes • masking tape
old jewelry • pompoms • rickrack • rug scraps • stick-on dots • yarn
needle and thread or fabric glue

Steps

- Pull the sock over the nondrawing hand, positioning the heel of the sock over the thumb. See how the puppet "talks" as the thumb and other fingers are pulled together and apart.
- Decide how to decorate the puppet making good use of the mouth of the sock puppet in the design.
- Begin sewing or gluing on scraps and other materials to give the puppet eyes, nose, hair, and personality.
- When done, help the puppet talk by opening and closing the puppet's mouth with a hand inside the sock.

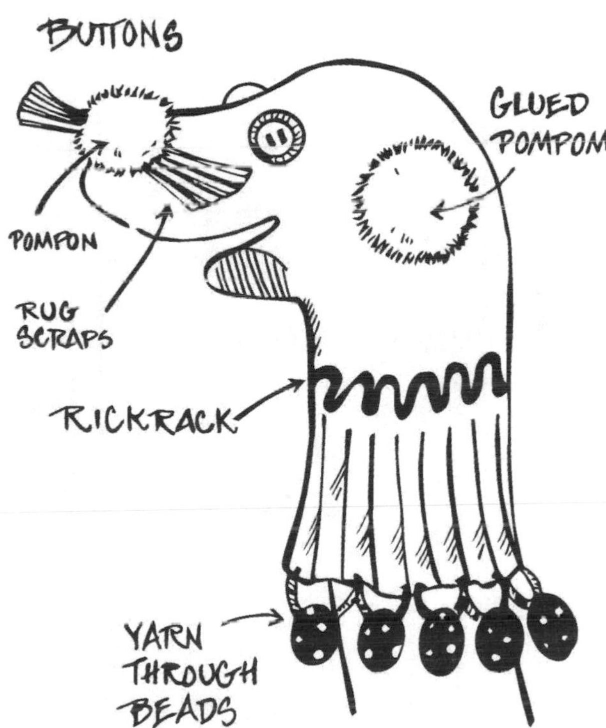

More Ideas

Stuff the toe of a sock with a ball of cotton stuffing or tissue paper. Tie a piece of string around the neck (not too tight). The rest of the sock is the puppet's body. Glue or sew on decorations as desired. Insert fingers in the head of the puppet.

As with all puppets, make up an original story, or act out a favorite book or fairy tale. Puppets can sing along with a favorite recording.

Doorway Stage

Combine creativity and easy storage with this puppet stage.

Materials

spring-tension curtain rod to fit a doorway
old sheet, table cloth, beach towel, or window curtain
sewing machine (adult managed)
scissors
newspapers
fabric pens
glue paints (tacky glue and tempera paints mixed together)
glitter, optional (add glitter to glue paints for sparkly look)
paintbrushes
rubber band, ribbon, or string

Steps

- With adult help, cut an old sheet or plain tablecloth to twice the width of a door—approximately 2 yards (2 m). Sew a simple casing along the long top edge large enough for the tension rod to be inserted—approximately 2″ (5 cm).
- Cover a table with newspapers. Spread the fabric on the papers.
- Design a glamorous curtain by painting with glue paints. Fabric pens are good for words, signs, and outlines. Dry completely.
- Feed the decorated curtain onto the spring-tension rod. Spread the spring-tension rod with curtain in a doorway at a height suitable for young puppeteers.
- Puppeteers crawl behind the curtain and put on a show.
- To store, roll up the curtain on the rod and slip into a shelf or closet until needed again. Hold with a rubber band, ribbon, or piece of string.

Body Puppet

1

Create a full body puppet to dance with or to use in a story.

Materials

sheet of paper, larger than child
crayons or markers
paints and brushes
scissors
masking tape, string, or rubber bands, optional

Steps

- Spread the paper on the floor.
- The child should lie down on the paper, face up, arms and legs somewhat extended with space around them. Posing in a funny position can be fun too.
- Draw an outline around the child's entire body.
- The child then paints or colors the body shape to be anyone they wish.
- Cut out the body shape, then cut holes for the eyes.
- The child holds the body puppet up in front of herself and pretends to be the voice of the puppet.

Hint: The puppet may need a little masking tape, string, or rubber bands to hold so the puppeteer can control the large body shape.

More Ideas

Create a series of full-sized characters.
Glue wallpaper to the body for clothes, then cut out the body shape.
Act out original stories, favorite books, nursery rhymes, or fairy tales.
Dance to music with the Body Puppet.

★★ 1 GLUE

Box Puppet

Don't throw away milk cartons, shoeboxes, or paper towel tubes. Make them into animals and people!

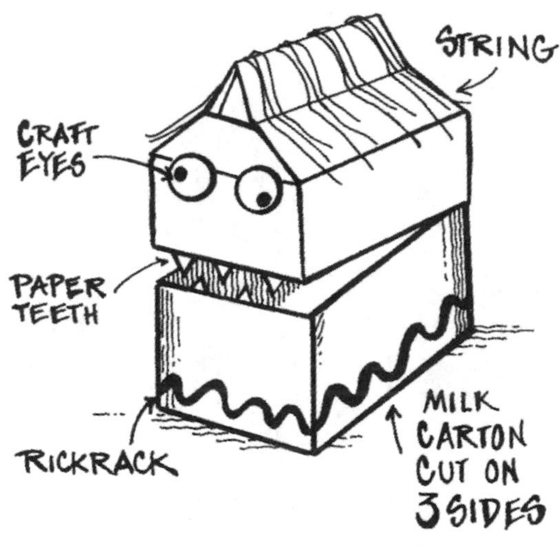

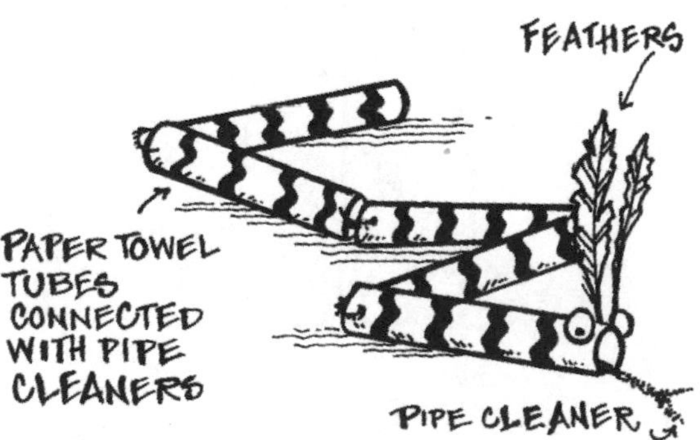

Materials

milk carton, shoebox, egg carton, or paper towel tube
glue
string, tape, scissors, stapler
odds and ends, such as
  buttons • feathers • paper scraps
  pipe cleaners • rickrack • sewing trim

Steps

- The illustrations show a few suggestions for making puppets with boxes and odds and ends.
- Create an animal puppet, such as a horse, bird, rabbit, or caterpillar. Or create a character from a story such as Three Billy Goats Gruff or Hansel and Gretel.
- Decorate, glue, staple, and assemble the puppet in any way, using the illustrations for ideas, or think up new ones.
- Put on a puppet show, act out a story, or become a new singing group.

More Ideas

Use other materials as the base for puppets, such as
  coffee can • egg beater • jewelry boxes • paper bag
  plastic liter bottle • ruler • soup can • Styrofoam block

Painted Hand Puppet

1 ★★

Materials

face paints or nontoxic paints that peel or wash off easily, such as BioColor
any puppet theater (easy suggestion: turn a table on its side and crouch down behind it)
soap and water, old towel

THE EASIEST AND MESSIEST HAND PUPPETS YOU CAN MAKE ARE RIGHT AT THE ENDS OF YOUR ARMS....YOUR HANDS!

Steps

- Decide whether to make each finger into a puppet, making five puppets, or to make the entire hand into one puppet. Decorate fingers or hand as a puppet (see illustration). See how the hand can be a full-face view or a side view. Notice how each finger can be a different character.
- Put on a show with any puppet theater.
- When done, wash hands in soapy water and dry with an old towel. Sometimes paints can take a day or two to completely wear off.

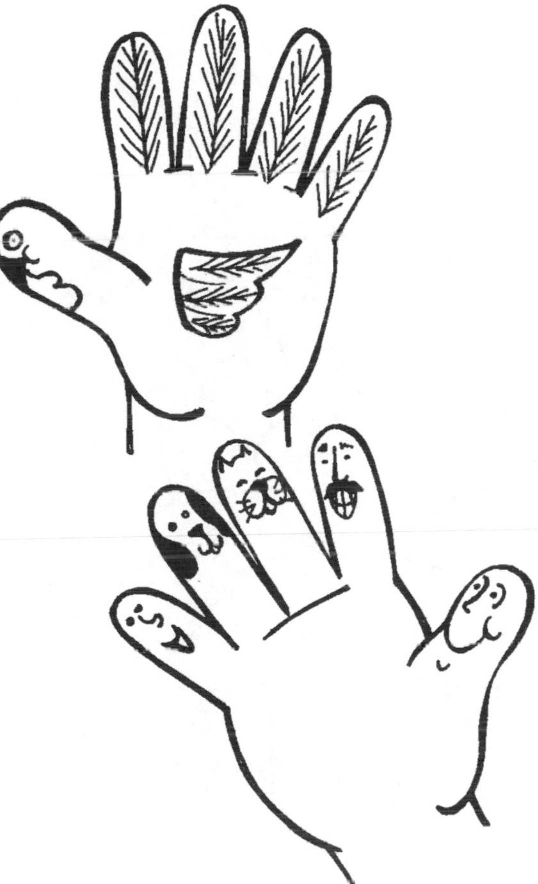

More Ideas

To dress the hand puppet, create a "Sleeve Costume" by cutting the sleeve off an old shirt. Secure it with a rubber band or piece of tape around the wrist. The sleeve will end near the elbow.

Enjoy watching the hand or finger puppets in a mirror.

Decorate a friend's hand, then put on a show together.

Tennis Ball Puppet

USE A FEW SIMPLE MATERIALS TO MAKE AN OLD TENNIS BALL INTO A FUNNY PUPPET ON A STICK.

Materials

old tennis ball (or Styrofoam, Ping-Pong, Nerf balls)
hot-glue gun, optional (adult only)
pointed scissors or screwdriver (adult only)
scrap of cardboard to cut for hands
wooden dowel approximately ½″ x 18″ (1 cm x 45 cm)
scissors
heavy piece of string approximately 12″ (30 cm) long
tape, glue, stapler
decorating materials, such as
buttons • cardboard scrap • colored telephone wire • corks
googly craft eyes • old doll clothes • paper scraps • permanent markers
pipe cleaners • ribbon • stickers • yarn

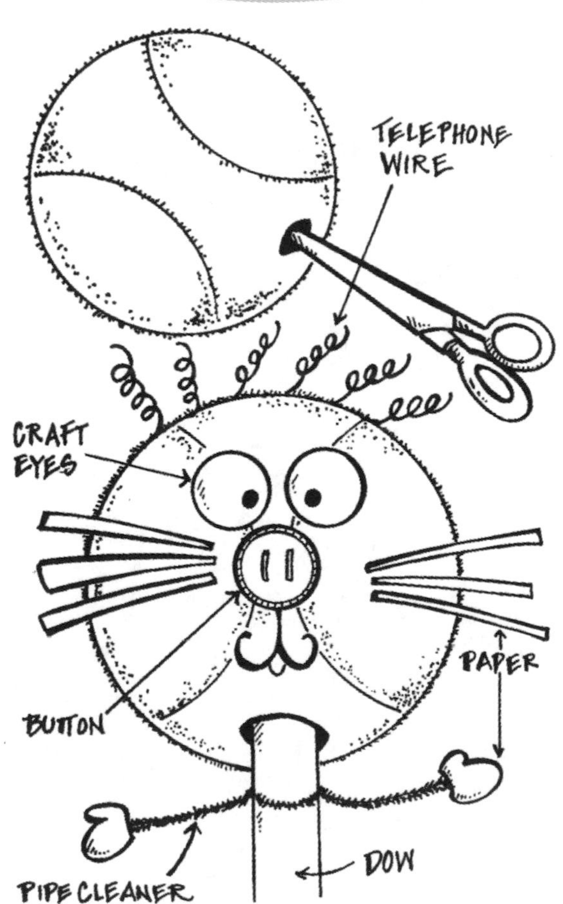

Steps

- An adult carefully pokes a hole smaller than the dowel in the tennis ball with the points of the scissors or some other cutting tool. Insert the end of the dowel into the hole in the tennis ball.

NOTE: FOR EXTRA STRENGTH, FIRST COVER THE TIP OF THE DOWEL WITH HOT GLUE AND THEN INSERT IT INTO THE BALL. SEAL THE HOLE IN THE BALL AROUND THE DOWEL WITH HOT GLUE. THE BASIC PUPPET IS READY FOR THE CHILD TO DECORATE.

- Create a puppet face! Select decorating materials to design a puppet's face on the tennis ball. Glue on items or draw features with markers. Add yarn for hair, if desired. A hat, beard, glasses, or any other imaginative ideas can be created from scrap materials.
- For wiggly arms, tie a piece of heavy string around the puppet stick a few inches below the face. Tie it nice and tight!

NOTE: A DROP OF HOT GLUE ON THE KNOT OF THE STRING WILL HELP HOLD IT SECURELY.

- Cut cardboard shapes for hands and glue them to the ends of the strings. If you cut four hand shapes, two pieces can be glued together over the ends of the string. When the puppet is acting and talking, the arms will wiggle and swing the heavy hands around.
- Let the show begin!

Crazy Kitchen Gadget Puppets

CREATE A WOODEN SPOON GIRL, DISH SCRUBBER MONSTER, SMALL SAUCEPAN ALIEN, SOUP LADLE SEA CREATURE, PAPER TOWEL TUBE GIRAFFE, OR NAPKIN GHOST WITH DISCARDED KITCHEN TOOLS.

Materials

used gadget or kitchen tool, such as
dish scrubber brush (with handle) • eggbeater • napkin • paper towel tube
soup ladle • wooden spoon

NOTE: CHECK GARAGE SALES FOR GREAT INSPIRATIONAL IDEAS!

materials for decorating, such as
art tissue paper • beads • buttons • embroidery floss • fabric scraps • glitter glue
googly craft eyes • hobby gems • magazine pictures • markers • paints and brushes
paper scraps • Ping-Pong balls • pompoms • sequins • sewing trims • stickers
wallpaper scraps • yarn

materials for attaching decorations and features, such as
duct tape • glue • masking tape • needle and thread • rubber bands
stapler • string • tape • wire • scissors

hot glue-gun, optional (adult only)

Steps

- Choose a gadget or tool that would make an interesting imaginary puppet character. The puppet does not have to be a person or an animal; it can be something that is completely imaginary and pretend.
- Assemble materials for decorating.
- Sew or glue on materials to design a puppet (see illustration). Think up your own—the possibilities are endless!

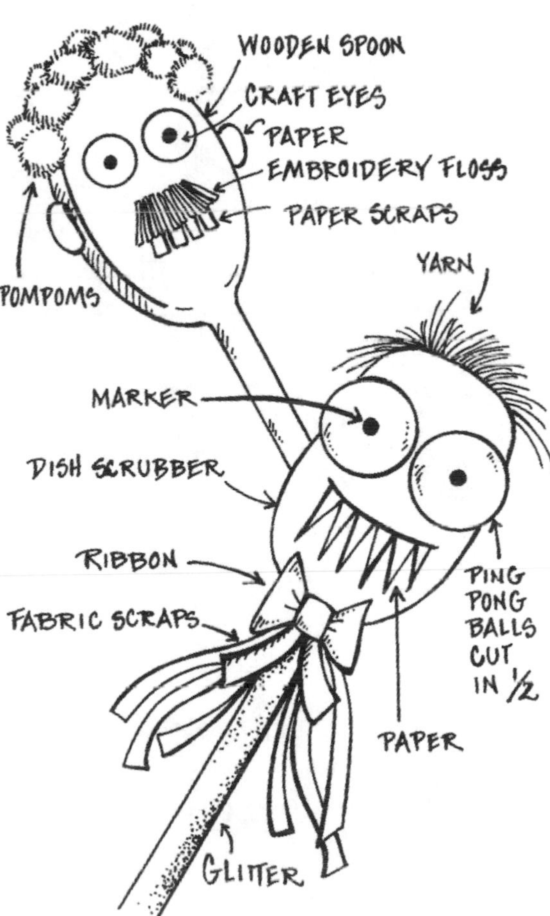

More Ideas

Make up a story about "life in the kitchen," that the kitchen tool puppets tell.
Add props to the puppet show like a frying pan, toaster (no cord), and silverware.

Simple Shadow Show

SHADOWS FROM CUT-OUT PAPER SHAPES TAPED TO DRINKING STRAWS ARE CAST TO THE BACK OF A LARGE SHEET OF PAPER TAPED TO A HOLE IN A PIECE OF CARDBOARD.

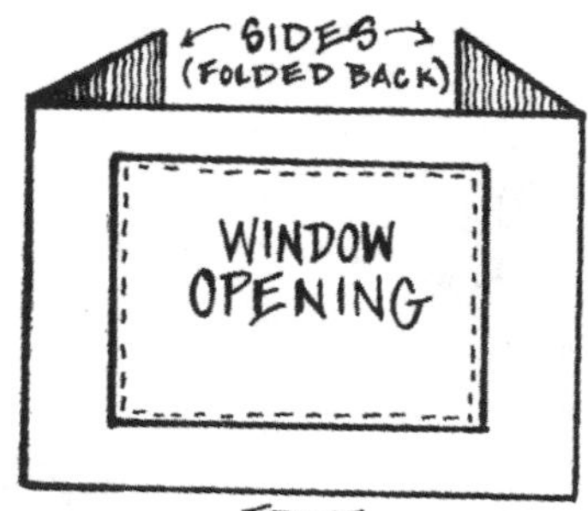

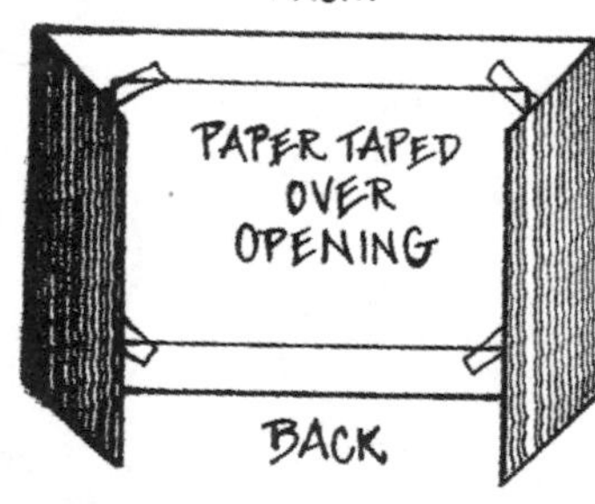

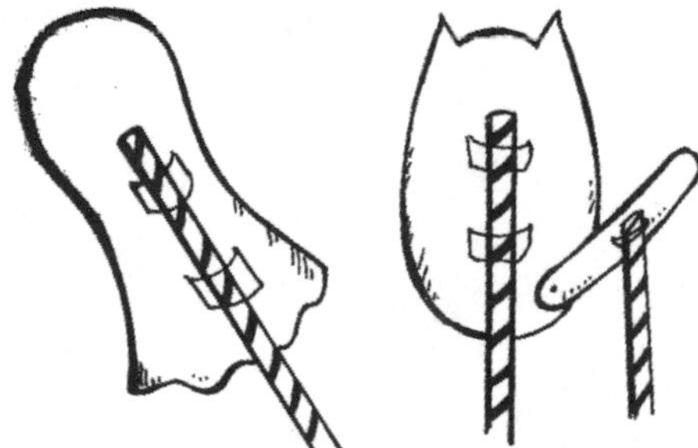

Materials

heavy paper or poster board
sticks or straws
tape
scissors
hole punch
paper fasteners
34″ x 18″ (approx. 1 m x .5 m) sheet of cardboard
large white paper 36″ x 20″ (1 m x .5 m)
craft knife (adult only)
table top
table lamp
sheet or blanket to drape table

Steps

To make the puppets

- For the easiest kind of puppet, draw a character on the heavy paper and cut it out. Attach a drinking straw "handle" to the back of the puppet with tape.
- For a movable puppet, cut out the puppet parts separately. With a hole punch, punch a hole in the movable part and also on the puppet body. Then join them with a paper fastener. Each movable part will have a drinking straw handle taped to it so it can be moved separately from the rest of the main puppet. Some ideas are
  - a tail that wags
  - arms and legs that wave or walk
  - head that moves
  - wings that flap

To make the shadow stage

- Fold the cardboard back 10″ (25 cm) from each side. This will make three panels: two side panels and one large center panel (see illustration).
- An adult carefully cuts out a large window in the center panel with a craft knife.
- Cut a large piece of white paper to at least an inch or two (3-5 cm) larger than the window in the cardboard. Place the panel face down on a table and tape the paper over the window.
- Stand the panel up on a tabletop that has been draped with an old sheet or blanket. Place a table lamp without a shade on the floor behind the stage. Dim other lights.
- Perform puppets against the white paper making shadow stories. Perform favorite stories or fairy tales, or make up original stories.

Thread Puppet

GLUE 2

THE THREAD PUPPET, SIMILAR TO A MARIONETTE, NEEDS ONLY ONE THREAD AND SOME RUBBER BANDS TO MAKE IT DANCE AND JIGGLE.

Materials

circle to trace, such as pop can or juice glass
pencil
2 large rubber bands
construction paper or poster board scraps
sticky dots
thread and toothpick
scissors, glue, tape, stapler, and crayons
quarter
cardboard box open at the top and front (see illustration)
fabric scraps for a curtain, optional

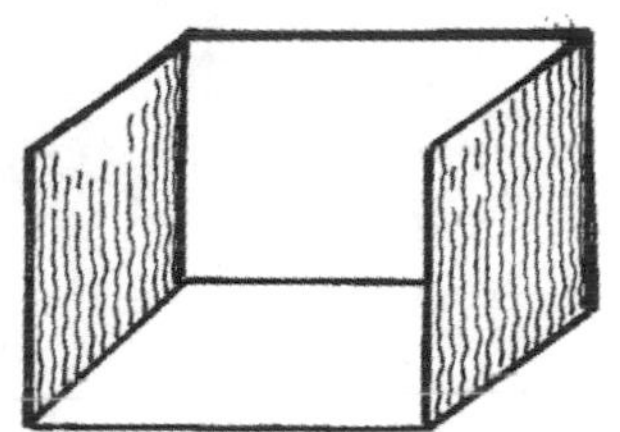

Steps

- The body of the puppet will be two circles. With a pencil, trace a circle on poster board. Cut out the two circles. Tape the circles together like a snowman, one for the head and one for the body.
- Snip each rubber band in half. Tape all four pieces to the body circle for arms and legs. Add hands and feet made from sticky dots stuck together at the ends of the rubber bands.
- Decorate the puppet with crayons or scraps of paper, adding facial features, hair, clothes, or whatever you choose.
- Tape a quarter to the back of the puppet for weight.
- Tape a thread to the back of the puppet's head. Press the tape down well to hold the thread. Tie the loose end of the thread to a toothpick or any small piece of wood or cardboard for a handle.
- Set up the cardboard box to act as a stage, with the top and front open. An adult may need to cut away some cardboard to make the stage. Staple some fabric scraps to the sides of the stage to look like a curtain, if desired.
- Suspend the puppet by its thread through the top of the box and bounce and jiggle it to make it dance and move.
- Construct more puppets as needed for a puppet show or to act out a favorite story.

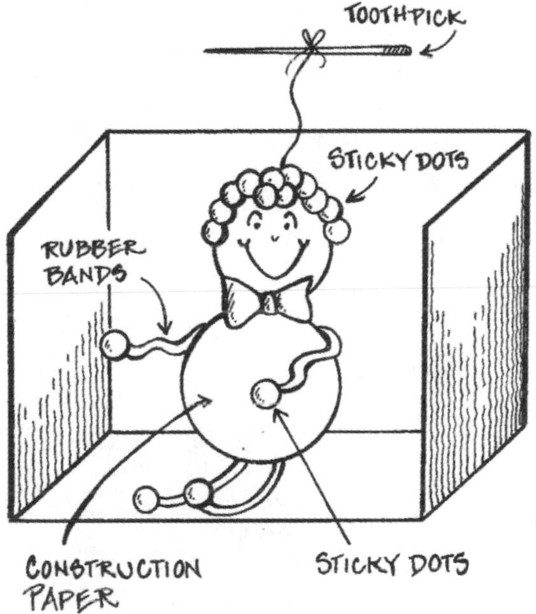

Soft Ol' Nightie Night Puppet

RECYCLE A SOFT OLD UNDERSHIRT OR DIAPER INTO A BEDTIME PUPPET STUFFED WITH FABRIC SCRAPS AND SEWN TOGETHER BY HAND.

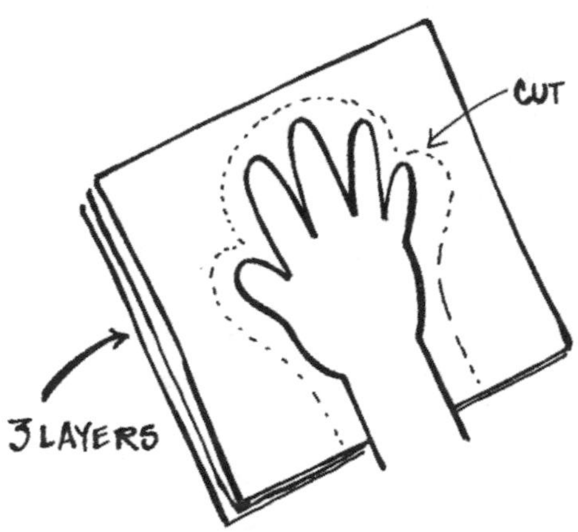

Materials

soft old piece of cotton fabric (undershirt, old diaper), enough for each of three layers to fit over one child-sized hand
permanent marker
scissors
needle and thread
stuffing material (scraps from the old undershirt work well)
optional materials for puppet features, like yarn for hair and buttons for eyes

Steps

- Spread the fabric or shirt on a table. There should be two layers of fabric, so double if necessary. If using an old undershirt, cut away all the collars, cuffs, and arms and use the remaining pieces of the front and back of the shirt for the puppet.
- Draw a bold, simple puppet shape with the permanent marker on the top layer of fabric by tracing around a child's hand. Leave extra room around the hand (see illustration). Puppet arms can be drawn in or left out completely.
- Cut through the doubled fabric, just outside the drawn lines.
- Trace this cutout on a third layer of fabric. Match all three layers in a stack.
- Sew the sides together by hand through all three layers at once, leaving a hole at the bottom for stuffing, and for holding the puppet later on.
- Stuff fabric scraps or other stuffing material into the front two layers of the puppet. When puffy and soft, sew the hole at the bottom closed through the front two layers only, leaving the third back layer free.

NOTE: THE EDGE OF THE THIRD LAYER CAN BE TURNED AND STITCHED, BUT CAN ALSO BE LEFT RAW EDGED. THE CHILD'S HAND WILL SLIP BETWEEN THE SECOND AND THIRD LAYERS.

- Draw facial characteristics or other decorations on the puppet with the permanent marker. Other features can be sewn to the puppet like yarn for hair and buttons for eyes, but are not necessary.
- Slip a hand in between the second and third layers, where the Nightie-Night Puppet is still open. Nightie-Night puppet might say, "Time for bed! Give me a hug! Please read me a story! Nightie-Night, I'm sleepy!"

Felt Board Storytelling

WHAT AN AMAZING FORM OF STORYTELLING A FELT BOARD CAN BE! PREPARE A FEW FAVORITE STORY CHARACTERS, AND USE THEM OVER AND OVER FOR MANY DIFFERENT STORIES, ORIGINAL OR WELL-REMEMBERED.

Materials

square of heavy cardboard or plywood approximately 36″ x 24″ (1 m x 60 cm)
large piece of felt to cover the board
fabric glue
old paintbrush
scissors
tape or stapler, optional
heavy, stiff interfacing fabric (ask at a fabric store)
permanent markers, variety of colors
pictures of characters to trace (from books or freehand)
colored pencils

Steps

To make the felt board

- Paint glue over the entire board. Use enough glue to soak into the felt. Don't forget to coat the edges of the board with glue too.
- Pull the felt tight across the board, pressing it into the glue and smoothing out wrinkles. Pull the edges of felt around to the back of the board and glue. Tape or staple the felt to the back as needed, then dry.
- Lean the board against a wall or use flat on the rug.

To make the felt board puppets

- Spread out the heavy interfacing on the table.
- Draw or trace a character on the interfacing. Use pencil, then outline with permanent markers. (Hold up to a window to trace designs.) Trace characters or draw them freehand. From Snow White to the kitten next door, all ideas are great for felt board puppets.
- Color the drawing or tracing with colored pencils or permanent markers.
- The interfacing puppets will easily cling to the felt-covered board.
- Play with the puppets on the board, telling and acting out stories. If desired, tell a story to others using the felt board puppets to act it out.

REMEMBER: A WOLF FOR LITTLE RED RIDING HOOD CAN ALSO BE THE WOLF FOR THE THREE PIGS AND THE GINGERBREAD MAN. MIX, MATCH, AND REUSE PUPPETS FOR DIFFERENT STORIES.

Cuddly Monster Puppets

MADE FROM COLORFUL ONE-SIZE WINTER GLOVES AND YARN, THESE CUDDLY MONSTER PUPPETS ARE A RAINBOW OF PRETEND FUN.

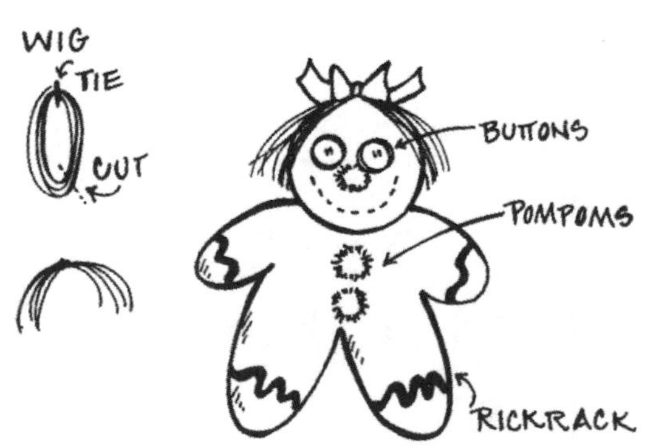

Puppet Materials

one-size-fits-all winter gloves, solid colors or patterns
needle and thread
Ping-Pong ball (or rubber ball)
rice or other stuffing
scissors
tacky glue
materials for puppet features, like
buttons • googly craft eyes • sewing trims • small pompoms
yarn or ribbon for wig

Steps

To make the puppets

- To make two legs, tuck the ring finger (next to baby finger) inside the glove so it doesn't show. Sew the hole closed with needle and thread (adult help may be needed).
- Fill the body of the puppet with rice or some other stuffing that is loose, like beads. Tie a piece of yarn tightly just below the cuff.
- For the puppet's head, stuff a ball into the cuff of the glove and stitch the top of the cuff closed around the ball.
- For the puppet's hair, make a yarn or ribbon wig. One idea is to wrap a long strand of yarn continuously around the hand about 25-50 times to make a round loop. Slip off the hand and tie a piece of yarn through one end of the loop. Snip the loop at the other end. Sew the wig to the top of the puppet's head.
- For the puppet's facial features, sew on or glue on buttons or small craft pompoms for noses, eyes, and mouths. Hobby craft eyes are another glue-on choice. Use other collage items or sewing trim as desired.

and Stick Stage

Stage Materials

2 rocks, bricks, or heavy blocks to fit in shoeboxes
2 shoeboxes
newspaper
tape
table
dowel, broomstick, or yardstick at least 3′ (1 m) long

To make the stick stage

- To weight the box, wrap a brick or a rock with newspaper. Put it in a shoebox. Stuff more paper in the box so it doesn't move around. Put on the lid and tape the box closed securely. Do this for each box.
- With adult help, carefully poke a hole with the points of the scissors in each box as shown in the illustration. The hole should be a size to fit the dowel or other stick.
- Set the boxes up on the table with the holes in the boxes facing each other. Insert the dowel in one box's hole and then in the other so the stick goes from one box to the other.
- To put on the puppet show with the Cuddly Monster Puppets, pose the puppets on the stick in various ways, behind or in front, arms hanging on, sitting, leaning, and so on. Puppets can be reposed throughout the show.

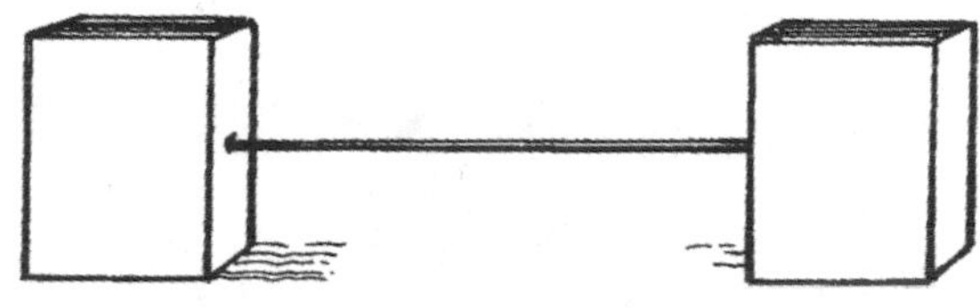

More Ideas

As with all puppets, make up a story or act out a familiar book or fairy tale.
Sing a progressive song like "The Ants Go Marching One by One" and change it to "The Monsters Go Marching One by One" with the puppets.
Assemble a group of puppets to sing a group song.

Lighted Box Stage with

TRANSFORM A SIMPLE CARDBOARD BOX INTO A PUPPET THEATER COMPLETE WITH REMOVABLE SCENERY AND STAGE LIGHTING FROM A FLASHLIGHT.

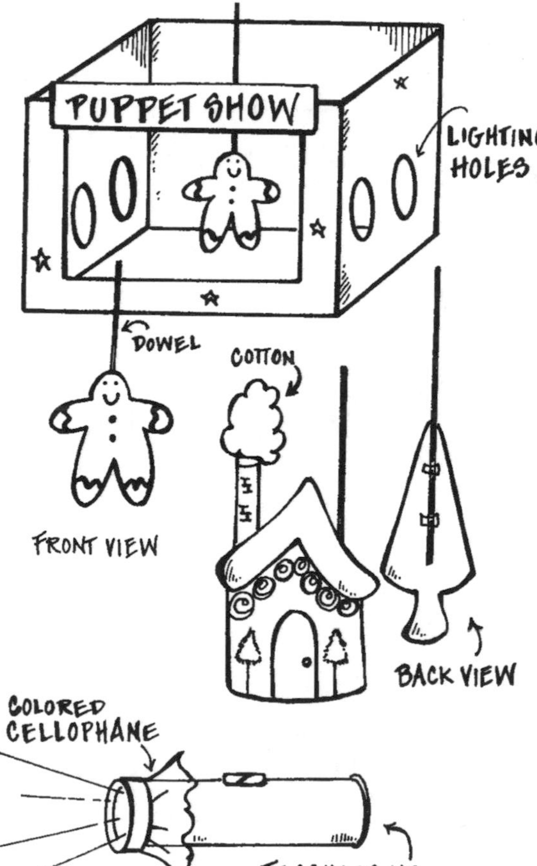

Materials

cardboard boxes, two the same size
(sturdy medium-sized boxes from wine or liquor bottles work well)
thin wooden sticks, such as
dowels • long bamboo skewers • wooden gardener's stakes
pencil
ruler
file cards for puppets
scissors
glue
paint and brushes
paper clips
masking tape and regular tape
flashlight
crayons or markers

Steps

To make the stage

- Select one box. Cut away the top flaps and save for scraps.
- Draw a stage opening on the front of the box, making a rectangle from the base approximately two-thirds of the way up. Make the opening fairly large, but leave some room on the sides to keep the stage sturdy (see the illustration). With adult help, cut out the piece.
- Paint the box inside and out with any chosen colors. Add painted decorations around the stage opening, if desired. Paint a sign for the puppet stage, like "Theater Magnificent," "Puppet Show," or "Eric's Best Stage Shows." Let dry completely.
- When dry, cut lighting holes in the sides of the theater. During a show, shine a flashlight through the holes to spotlight a puppet. A lighted show may take two or more people to perform.

Stick Puppets

To make the scenery and puppets

- With cardboard from the second box and flap scraps, draw and paint scenery for the puppet stage. When dry, cut the scenery out with adult help. Depending on the story, scenery might include a cottage, trees, or the inside of a house.
- The scenery will hang from the sticks into the stage area. Tape the top of each piece of scenery to a long thin stick. Make each stick longer than the width of the box so it will rest on the top of the box.
- Cut little nicks in the left and right top edges of the box for the sticks to rest in so the scenery hangs down into the stage area.
- Now draw and color several puppet characters on the file cards. Cut them out. Trace the puppets on a second card and color these for the backs of the puppets.
- Glue each front and back of the puppet to a stick. Be sure the stick comes out of the puppet's head upward. Hold until the glue sticks (see illustration). Tape an opened paper clip to the top of the stick to work as a hook and a handle.
- To perform with the stick puppets, insert the puppets on their sticks through the ceiling of the stage and perform amidst the scenery. When puppets are not moving but must remain on stage, they can hang by their hooks from the scenery sticks.

More Ideas

Cover the flashlight with colored cellophane held in place with a rubber band to change the lighting to different colors and effects.

Design puppets from a special storybook or fairy tale, or make up a story.

Attach small toys or other items such as toy cars, animals, dinosaurs, or doll furniture on the sticks to use as puppets or props.

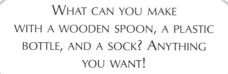

Spoonhead Bottle Dolls

What can you make with a wooden spoon, a plastic bottle, and a sock? Anything you want!

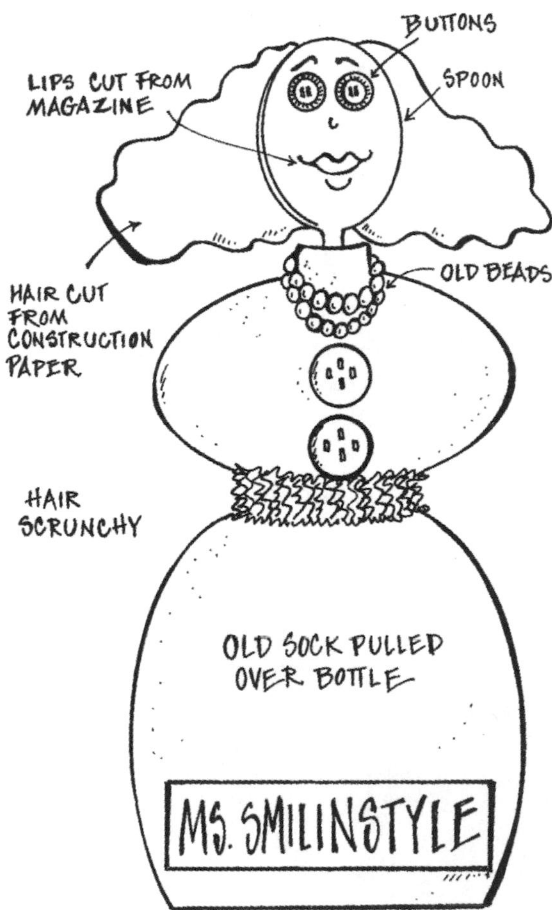

Materials

plain white cotton sock
plastic bottle, as from
 bottled water • dishwashing liquid •soda pop
short-handled wooden spoon
decorating supplies, such as
 buttons • construction paper • earrings • glue • hair scrunchies • markers
 old bracelets • old magazines • photographs • rubber bands • yarn

Steps

- Turn the sock inside out. Stuff the toe into the bottle. Then turn the rest of the sock right side out, gently pulling it around the bottle to make the doll's body. Now the doll looks like it is wearing a sweater or dress.
- For the face of the doll, stick the handle of the wooden spoon into the bottle. The bowl of the spoon will look like the doll's head. (If the handle is too long, cut it shorter or use a shorter spoon.)
- Draw facial features with markers on the spoon. Or, cut eyes and a mouth from magazine pictures and glue them on the spoon. Glue on construction paper ears, if desired.
- For the hair, cut construction paper into strips and glue on the spoon, or glue pieces of yarn in place to look like hair.
- Accessorize the doll with old jewelry such as a bracelet used as necklace, earrings attached to the ears, buttons sewn on the sock, or hair scrunchies used as belts or collars. Use paper or sewing scraps in any way.

More Ideas

Help the Spoonheads make up a story or pantomime to a song.
Arrange the Spoonheads on a shelf or table. Give them paper signs and label them with silly names to match their personalities, such as
 Darling Dora • Fuzzyhead Freida • Ms. Smilinstyle

Doorway Shadow Screen with Stick Puppets

FASTEN AN OLD SHEET ACROSS A DOORWAY THAT'S NOT USED MUCH, SHINE A LIGHT ON THE SHEET TO MAKE A BRIGHT SHADOW SCREEN, AND ADD PAPER PUPPET SHAPES.

Materials

old sheet
heavy fabric such as
 beach towel • tablecloth • light blanket
doorway not in use
masking tape or pushpins
desk lamp on a stool or table
heavy paper for puppets
narrow dowels or bamboo skewers for puppet sticks
crayons or markers
scissors
stapler, optional

Steps

- Tape or pin a sheet to cover a doorway that is not used often. Leave the bottom of the sheet free for puppeteers to climb in and out.
- Tape or pin a heavier piece of fabric across the lower half of the doorway, again leaving the bottom free for a puppeteer's entrance.
- Set up a desk lamp on a stool or table behind the screen, higher than the head of a puppeteer on his knees. This will keep the shadow of the head out of the performance area. Shine the light on the sheet.

NOTE: CREATE SPECIAL EFFECTS, SUCH AS MAKING THE PUPPET LOOK VERY LARGE, BY MOVING THE LIGHT TOWARDS THE SCREEN OR AWAY FROM THE SCREEN.

- To make the puppets, cut shapes of characters from heavy paper or cardboard. The puppet will be a silhouette, so additional decorations or features are not necessary. Only the shape of the puppet will be seen.
- Tape the puppet shapes to bamboo skewers. Additional stapling may be necessary to make the puppets strong. Remember that the tape and staples will not show, so don't be worried about using as much as necessary to create strong puppets.
- Hold the puppets up above the heavy fabric, moving and making them perform with light shining on them. The audience on the other side of the shadow screen will see a show of shadowy shapes acting out stories or dancing.

More Ideas

Design a puppet with movable arms or legs attached with metal fasteners. Attach additional skewers or sticks to the arms and legs to control them and make them move.

3 Favorite Table Theater

Tape scenery to a table on its side, then crouch behind it. Let the play begin!

Materials

table (school table, card table, coffee table)
choices of other materials for decorating
sheet, fabric, or towel
paper, paper scraps, lightweight cardboard scraps
scissors
ruler, optional
markers, crayons, or paints with brushes
tape, pins, safety pins, stapler, or glue

Steps

- Turn a table on its side with the tabletop facing the audience. Crouch behind the table for a puppet theater.
- Suggestions to enhance the bare table with scenery or decor
  - Drape a sheet, towel, or fabric over the tabletop. Tape to the table's edges to secure.
  - Decorate the sheet with paper decor. Tape or pin to the table.
  - Paint a sign and tape it across the tabletop.
- Suggestions to make scenery
  - Paint or color scenery on heavy paper or cardboard. Cut out.
  - Tape to the edge of the table where puppets can be a part of the scene.
  - Scenery may need rulers or cardboard supports taped to the pieces to help them stand. Tape to the table edge.
- On with the show!

More Ideas

Other easy puppet theaters include standing behind
- a clothesline strung from one tree to another, draped with a sheet
- a bookshelf, using the top of the shelf for scenery and props
- a sofa or couch
- a curtain on a spring-tension rod in a doorway.

Story Apron

PUPPETS, HIDDEN IN DEEP POCKETS, WAIT THEIR TURNS TO PERFORM ON THIS UNUSUAL PUPPET STAGE.

Materials

any apron (see illustration)
fabric to make into pockets
sewing machine (adult managed) and thread or fabric glue
scissors
choice of puppets—Old Glove Finger Puppets, page 67; Cuddly Monster Puppets, page 80; and Finger Puppets, page 63 are good choices for puppets in pockets.

Steps

To make the story apron

- Cut a long rectangle of fabric approximately 1 yd. x 12″ (1 m x 30 cm) to reach across the entire front of the apron, from left to right, along the hem line of the apron. If sewn, turn the edges under and sew the big rectangle pocket to the apron front (see illustration). If gluing, follow the same placement directions, then dry.
- Next, sew from the hem line to the top of the pocket, making individual pockets about 6″ (15 cm) wide or large enough to reach a hand comfortably inside. Make at least four pockets.
- Now cut another long rectangle about 1 yd. x 6″ (1 m x 15 cm). Sew or glue this long strip above the first pockets. Sew these into individual pockets too.

To use the story apron

- Put on the story apron.
- Choose puppets for a story to tell. For this example, gather a little girl in a red cape, a wolf, a grandmother, and a woodcutter to tell the story of Little Red Riding Hood. Place them in order in the deep pockets where they cannot be seen.
- Stand to tell the story. Begin by bringing out Little Red Riding Hood and place her in a shallow pocket, or hold her up for all to see. Tell about how she wanted to visit her grandmother in the forest. As she walks along through a pretend invisible forest, bring out the wolf from a deep pocket with the free hand. When the wolf leaves, he can go back into

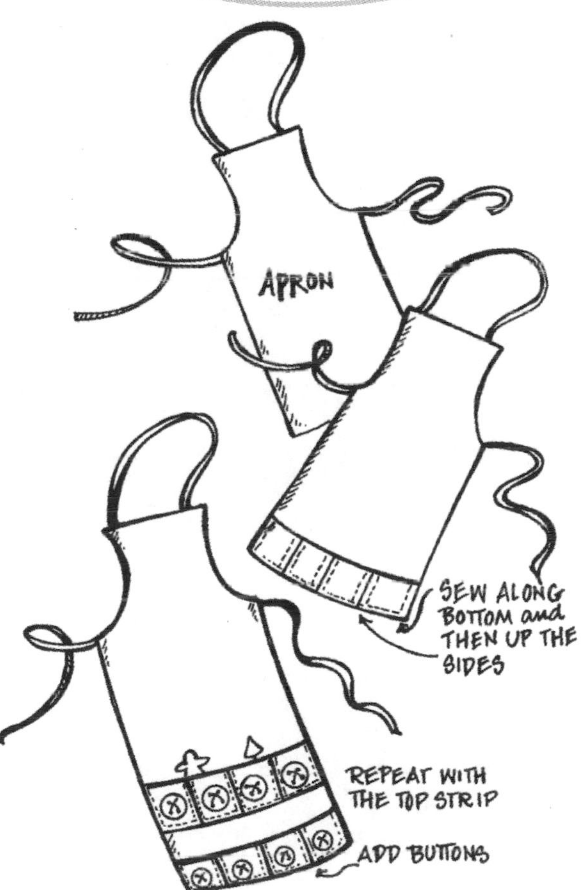

the pocket. Later, when Red Riding Hood reaches her grandmother's house, have the grandmother come out of the pocket. Active characters can be held by hand. Less active characters can rest in the shallow pockets, and inactive characters can go back into hidden deep pockets.

- Apron Storytelling is great fun and produces much excitement because of the thrill of knowing that a wolf or troll or silly friend is hiding, waiting to come out.

More Ideas

Sew big buttons on the apron front. Tie or sew loops of ribbon or yarn to puppets heads for the storytelling time. Hang them from the buttons while "on-stage" instead of going into pockets to await their turns. Remove the loops when puppets return to other stages or uses.

Hats, Costumes & Masks

Chapter 4

1

My Hat Collection

Collect hats, caps, bonnets, helmets, and more from garage sales and second-hand stores for the easiest and best creative play.

Materials

collect real hats from garage sales or second-hand stores, such as
bike helmet • captain's hat • cowboy hat • fancy ladies' hat • farmer's straw hat
fast food paper hat • firefighter's helmet • hard hat • safari hat • sailor hat • ski hat
sun visor • surgeon's cap • watch cap

several storage suggestions (try just one at a time)
cardboard box • clean trash can • clothespins on clothes hangers • clothespins on clothesline • clothespins on fishnet on the wall • coat hooks on wall

hat cubbies: shoeboxes stacked and taped together • plastic bin • safety pin on each hat as a hanger • standing hat rack

Velcro Hat Rack (see page 101)

Steps

- Start with just one or two hats. Add more or take some away as time goes on.
- Put on a hat, and begin the pretending!
- When done, return hats to storage areas.

Note: Hats from garage sales should be cleaned before being used in creative play.

10 Easy Hats to Make

1

With paper and cardboard, create any or all of these ten easy hats, such as crown, bonnet, headdress, or clown.

Materials

materials for the bases of hats, such as
box • egg carton • hair band • heavy paper • lightweight cardboard • milk carton
newspaper • panty hose • paper bag • paper plate • poster paper • wool watch cap
glue, stapler, tape, scissors
drawing tools: crayons, markers, paint and brushes
collage and decorative materials, such as
aluminum foil • art tissue scraps • beads • bows • buttons • confetti • corks • cotton balls
crepe paper • curled paper • feathers • felt scraps • glitter • hobby gems • pipe cleaners
pompoms • ribbons • sequins • sewing trim • yarn • zippers

Steps

Headband style

Cut a 3″ (8 cm) wide strip of lightweight cardboard or heavy paper long enough to go around the head plus a little more for overlapping. Staple to hold. Add decorations to the headband to create the suggestions below, or think up others!

❶ Bunny Ears
Cut two long ears from white paper, color them pink in the middle, and staple to band. Hop! Hop! Other animal ear suggestions: wolf, donkey, elephant.

❷ Regal Crown
Cut the band in a zigzag pattern and decorate with hobby jewels, foil, glitter, sequins, and sewing trims

❸ Visor Hat (Zoo Keeper, Police Officer, Painter)
Cut an additional piece of cardboard in a half circle as the visor and tape to the front of the band. Decorate as desired.

❹ Straw Hat
Attach a circle of paper to the headband. Paint or add decorations such as plastic fruit or flowers to make an Easter bonnet.

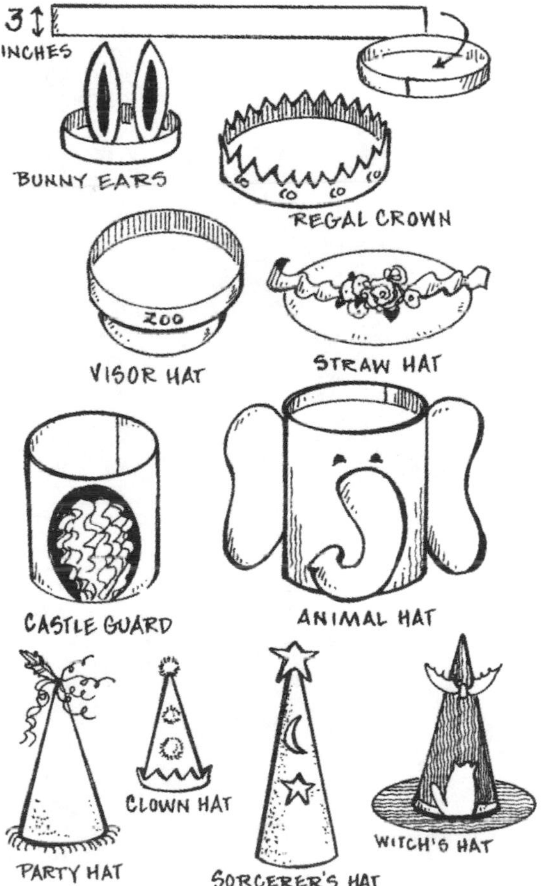

Tube style

Cut a wide piece of poster board or other stiff paper long enough to go around the head plus a little more for overlapping. Staple to hold.

❺ Castle Guard Hat
Make a wide tube, approximately 12″ (30 cm) tall. Decorate with ruffles of crepe paper.

❻ Animal Hat
Like the castle guard, make a wide tube. Draw animal features on the tube and wear this hat like a mask. Some effective animals for this hat are lion, rabbit, elephant, alligator, mouse, reindeer, dog, cat, monkey.

Cone style

Pull the edges of a large piece of paper together, forming a cone that will fit the head and tape securely. Snip off the uneven edges to make a straight line around the head. The cone base is the beginning of the following hat ideas, or think up more!

❼ Party Hat
Decorate the hat with glitter, feathers, sequins, and other sparkly, materials. Make several and celebrate the day.

❽ Clown Hat
Glue decorative items on the basic cone like pompoms and ribbons.

❾ Sorcerer's Hat
Cover with foil stars and moons.

❿ Witch's Hat
Make with black paper. Add a bright ribbon band and cat or bat cutouts.

More Ideas

Explore the creation of hats from paper bags, boxes, milk cartons, panty hose, egg cartons, and more. Experiment with your ideas.

Paper Plate Hats Workshop

WITH HEAVY PAPER PLATES, CREATE HATS FROM A TO Z AND 1 TO 100.

Materials

heavy duty paper plates
items to decorate paper plates
art tissue • beads • bows • buttons • cellophane • confetti • drinking straws
Easter grass • feathers • felt scraps • glitter • googly craft eyes • paper scraps
pipe cleaners • pompoms • curly ribbons • sequins • sewing trim • yarn
paste, glue, tape, stapler
markers, crayons
hole punch

Steps

- Set up a table with all the materials needed for making hats.
- Prepare the hat base. See the illustrations for examples. Suggestions include
  brim hat • headband hat • simple flat hat • tripod hat
- Start adding materials, attaching them with glue, tape, stapler, or tying them on the hat. Make simply silly hats, glitzy hats, crazy hats, character hats, or theme hats. Examples of character hats to make are
  crown • curly hair wig • elephant • outer space • princess
  Examples of theme hats to make are
  birthday • colors • flowers • holidays • rainbow • sunshine
- Wear the hats for dress-up, pretend, parades, or parties.

More Ideas

Substitute disposable aluminum pie pans for paper plates.

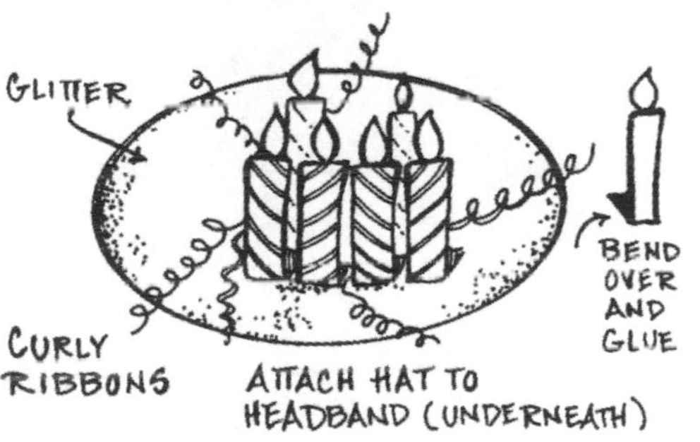

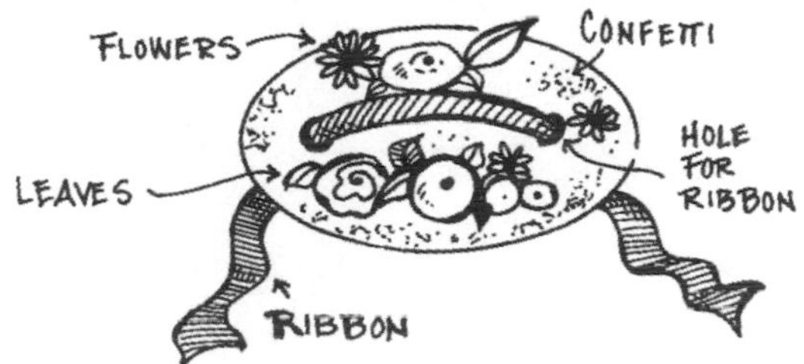

Easy Make-Up and Wigs

Here are some of the easiest, best suggestions for make-up and wig ideas you'll ever need. They are both easy-to-do and very convincing.

Materials

real cosmetics or face paints
brush or cotton swab
sponges
hand lotion
panty hose
scarf or towel
paper or plastic bag
scissors
paper scraps, fabric scraps, or ribbon
swimming cap
bows, yarn
rag mop
curling ribbon
stapler, tape, stapler
headband

Steps

Make-Up—3 ideas

- Real cosmetics are the best choice for make-up as they are generally gentle on the skin and easy to remove. For best removal, coat the face with a gentle facial lotion before applying make-up. With eyebrow pencil or eyeliner, draw features like mustaches, freckles, giant eyelashes, and extended mouths. Rouge, eye shadow, lipstick, and other colorings work beautifully. Remove with a gentle facial lotion or warm, soapy water.
- Face paints can be used directly on the skin. Draw gently and carefully. Wash with warm water and soap, or remove with a gentle facial lotion.

Wigs—7 ideas

❶ Panty Hose
Pull the hose over the hair like a hat, with legs hanging loose like bunny ears. Tuck hair inside the hose. Tie the legs at the top of the head. Legs resemble ears or hair as is, or can be decorated with yarn or paper to add curls or color.

❷ Scarf or Towel
A scarf or towel draped over the head resembles long hair. Tie with ribbon or a long piece of fabric like a headband.

❸ Paper Bag
Cut one side of the bag away. Leave a ridge of bangs, if desired. Cut the rest of the bag into fringe, curling it if desired. Pull the bag on over the head as a wig. Glue on paper scraps, fabric scraps, or curled ribbon to enhance the wig. A plastic bag or small garbage bag also works for this wig idea.

❹ Swimming Cap
Pull on a plain swimming cap to resemble a bald head. Leave completely bald, or decorate with extra hair around the ears with bows, curled ribbon, scraps of paper, or yarn.

❺ Rag mop
A clean rag mop makes a great wig. Tie clumps of the mop with yarn or ribbon to loop like ponytails or other hair design.

❻ Ribbon
Curl ribbon and tie or clip to real hair to look like curly hair.

❼ Headband
A cardboard circle stapled to fit around the head can have many different materials glued or stapled to it to look like hair.

1

Who Am I?

DRESS UP IN CLOTHING AND ACCESSORIES TO RESEMBLE SOMEONE FAMOUS, SOMEONE SPECIAL, A FAMILY MEMBER, OR A BEST FRIEND. THEN ASK, "WHO AM I?"

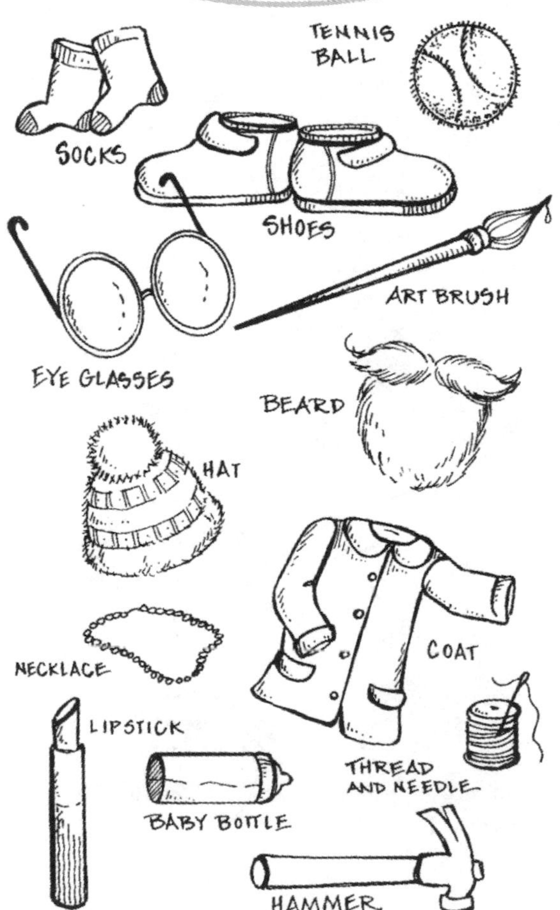

Materials

dress-up clothes, such as
boots • coat • dress • hat • pants • shirt • shoes • skirt • socks • sport clothes
dress-up accessories, such as
beard • freckles • glasses • jewelry • lipstick • make-up • ribbon, bow, hair band stuffing • wig
equipment for hobbies or interests, such as
arts • baby bottle • blanket • books • games • gardening tools hobbies • pacifier • pets • sports • tools

Steps

- Decide who to portray in dress-up costume. Think of everything that person might wear, carry, or use as accessories or make-up. For example, if dressing like a baby sister, carry a pacifier, bottle, and blanket. Wear pajamas with feet and pink rouge on the cheeks. If portraying a favorite football hero, wear a helmet, big shirt with a number, and black under the eyes.
- Dress like that character or person.
- Then ask, "Who am I?"
- Let everyone in on the act, dressing and guessing. From serious to silly, this is more than a game–it's a skill.

More Ideas

Put dress-up items in a box. Pull out a few random pieces and dress up in them. Then have everyone try to decide who the particular outfit makes you resemble.

Flipped Face

1 ★

THE OBJECT OF THIS SILLY UPSIDE DOWN FACE PAINTING IS AN OPTICAL ILLUSION THAT PRODUCES HYSTERICAL LAUGHTER FOR ADULTS AND CHILDREN.

Materials

face paint
bandanna or scarf
child's face (the model)
friend to paint (the artist)
cosmetic mirror

Steps

- The child whose face will be painted (the model) lies on his back with his head and neck resting just over the edge of a bed or table. His chin should be pointing up and his hair should be hanging down.
- The child who will be doing the painting (the artist) paints over the model's eyebrows with paint to hide them.
- Paint new eyebrows on the model's cheeks and a new mouth on the model's forehead. Add any other embellishments such as nostrils at the bridge of the nose, rosy cheeks where eyebrows used to be, or funny eyelashes as desired.
- For a final touch, tie a bandanna or scarf around the chin and neck to hide the real mouth of the model. Fluff out hair or brush it to look like a beard for the upside down face.
- Make faces; roll the eyes, smile, and frown. The fun is beginning! The model may want to look in a mirror to see what everyone is laughing at!
- Take turns being the model and the artist. Let everyone join the fun!

More Ideas

Recipe for Grease Paint

4 tablespoons shortening • 10 tablespoons cornstarch • 2 tablespoons flour • ¼ teaspoon glycerin • food coloring

On a flat smooth surface, blend shortening, cornstarch, and flour with a spatula to make a paste. Add glycerin and blend again. Mix divided portions with a few drops of food coloring each. Use fingers to apply to the face. To remove, use cold shortening and baby oil.

★ 1 GLUE !

Stocking Mask

CREATE A MAGICAL MASK FROM OLD NYLON STOCKING SCRAPS, SEWING TRIM, BUTTONS, AND OTHER DECORATIVE MATERIALS.

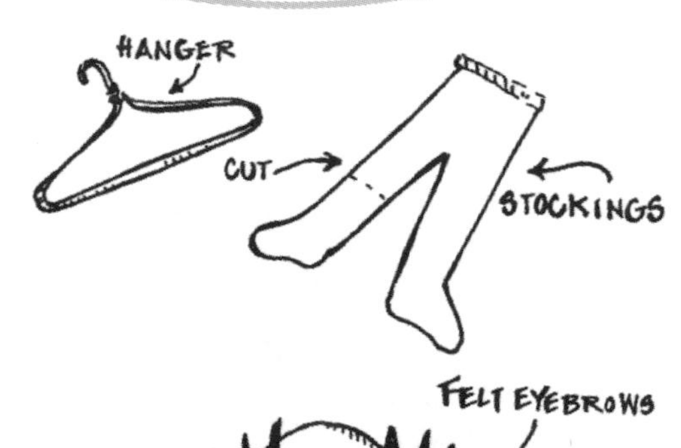

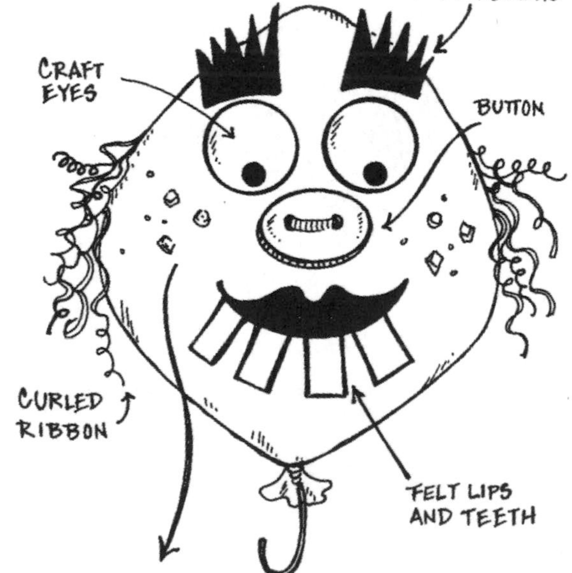

Materials

old, clean nylon stockings (panty hose work well)
wire coat hanger for each mask
scissors
yarn or string
optional scraps for decorating, such as
buttons • craft fur • curled ribbon • fabric scraps • felt scraps • glue
googly craft eyes • hobby gems • needle and thread • paper scraps • yarn

Steps

- Open and bend a wire coat hanger until it is rounded with the hook end like a handle (adult only, see illustration). Set aside.
- Cut one leg of the stocking in half across the knee.
- Pull the section with the foot over the rounded end of a wire coat hanger. Tie the other open end of the stocking around the handle of the coat hanger with string or yarn.
- To make a face and decorate the mask, sew, glue, or attach buttons, fabric, yarn, or other decorative materials to the stocking. Let dry.
- Hold the see-through stocking mask up in front of the face like holding a mirror.

More Ideas

Use a new voice.
Try out being a new you behind the mask. Some words to help:
be bold, not shy
be brave, not frightened
be indifferent, not caring
be old, not young
be dull, not wise

Face-Paint Stencils

2 ☆

FACE PAINTING IS ONE OF THE EASIEST WAYS TO CREATE A DISGUISE. MAKE IT EVEN EASIER WITH STENCILS.

Materials

face paint
make-up sponges, slightly damp
face lotion
paper
selection of brushes, like
  cotton swab • eyeliner brush
  make-up brush • small paintbrush
scissors
pie pan or other plate
mirror, optional
tape
pencil

Steps

- Cut a small design, shape, or other stencil from the paper. A bold design like a star, flower, or cat without a lot of detail works the best.
- If working alone, look in the mirror for the next steps. Or friends can paint friends.
- Hold the stencil on the forehead or cheek. Use a little tape to hold the stencil, if desired.
- Press the damp makeup sponge into a selected color of face paint. Dab it on the edge of the pan or on a scrap of paper to remove extra paint. Now gently dab the face paint on the stencil, covering the skin that shows through the stencil. Let dry a moment.
- Remove the stencil and the painted design will remain. The stencil can be used again, but is most effective the first time.
- Do as many stencil designs as desired. Explore the use of the brushes and swabs for outlining or mixing colors on the skin.
- When dry, remove paints with soap and water, or gently remove with face lotion and paper towels or tissues.

More Ideas

Paint designs without stencils on the face.
Paint the face to look like favorite animals, characters, or themes.

Foil Mask

Using aluminum foil from the kitchen, gently form a mask to make a metallic creature likeness that is most amazing!

Materials

sheet of kitchen aluminum foil, not heavy duty, about 12″ x 30″ (30 cm x 90 cm)
scissors or pencil
string, piece of elastic, or 1″ (3 cm) wide heavy paper band
tape, glue, stapler

Steps

Note: Adult supervision and help required.

- Fold the sheet of foil in half so it is now about 12″ x 15″ (30 cm x 40 cm).
- The child closes her eyes. An adult will gently mold the foil over the child's face, pressing the foil to mold to facial features. Ask the child to breathe comfortably.
- Keep the foil against the child's face and with hands gently tear nostril holes, mouth hole, and eye holes where needed. Remove and replace the foil off and on as needed while tearing holes. When holes are complete, remove the foil mask.
- Work to fold in the edges around the eyes, nose, and mouth for a more finished look.
- Take the mask off the child's face and, with scissors or a pencil, pole a hole at each side of the mask. Add string or a piece of elastic so the mask can be worn. Add tape to reinforce the holes. Be careful when putting the mask on or taking it off because the foil can tear easily.

Note: Staple a 1″ (3 cm) wide strip of heavy paper to the mask. This works like a headband instead of string or elastic.

- For a finishing touch, glue on more pieces of foil for additional features or details, or the mask can be enjoyed in its original form.

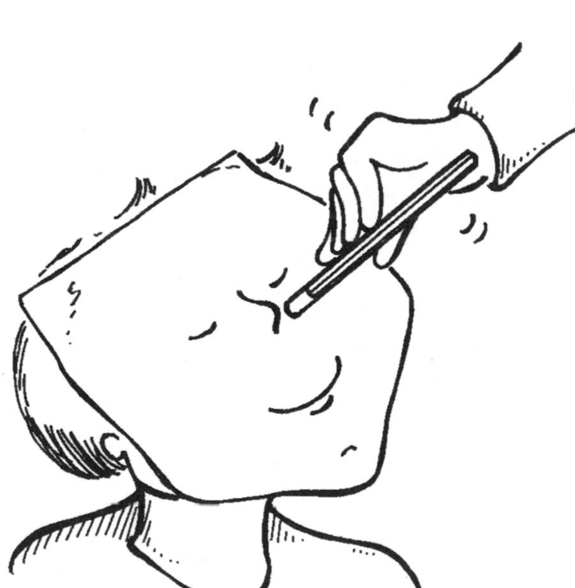

More Ideas

Staple, tape, or glue paper scraps, streamers, sewing trims, yarn, or other materials to the mask.

Velcro Hat Rack

CREATE A VELCRO HAT RACK TO KEEP PLAY HATS EASILY ACCESSIBLE FOR CREATIVE PLAY.

Materials

Velcro squares from fabric stores
fabric glue or needle and thread
glue or stapler
thin piece of wood, cup hooks, and wall screws or hammer and nails, optional
hats (see page 90 for suggestions)

Steps

- Sew or glue the "hook" part of the Velcro square to a hat, preferably to the rim or an edge. Attach the squares to all of the hats to be stored.
- For the easiest approach, glue or staple the other part of the Velcro square directly to the wall.
- For a more temporary or removable set-up, glue or staple the squares to a long, thin piece of wood like a flat piece of ceiling molding. Then, with adult help, the molding can be nailed or screwed to the wall (one nail at each end). It can also be hung from a few cup hooks placed at child height; loop some wire around each end of the board to hang from the hooks.
- Press the Velcro on each hat to the Velcro on the wall or wood. What a convenient storage idea for keeping hats tidy and organized!

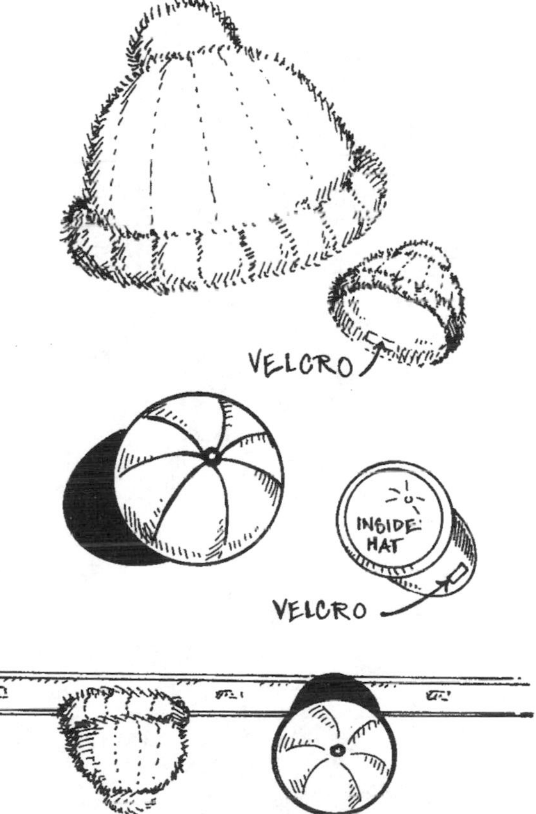

★★ 1

Egg Carton Nose

EVER WONDER WHAT TO DO WITH ALL OF THOSE EGG CARTONS? CREATE NOSES—FROM PIGS TO WOLVES, CATS TO DOGS, ALIENS TO MONSTERS, AND BARNYARDS TO JUNGLES.

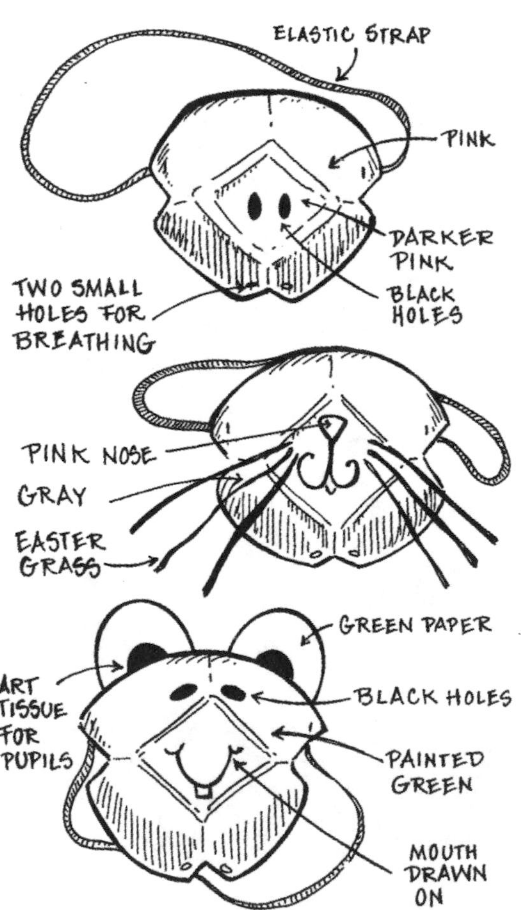

Materials

cardboard egg carton
elastic or other stretchy sewing trim (used in bathing suits and underwear)
paint and brushes
decorative materials, such as
  art tissue • beads • bows • buttons • cellophane • confetti • curly ribbons
  cut drinking straws • Easter grass • feathers • felt scraps • glitter • googly craft eyes
  paper scraps • pipe cleaners • pompoms • sequins • sewing trims • yarn
glue, stapler, tape
scissors

Steps

- Cut the cups apart from a cardboard egg carton. Each cup will be a nose.
- Cut holes in the bottom edge of each cup for easy breathing.
- Staple an elastic strip from one side of the nose to the other, measuring to fit comfortably around the head.
- Now the fun begins. Decorate the nose with pompoms, pipe cleaners for whiskers, paints, markers, and so on in whatever style and design suits the artist. Some suggestions are:
  - for an easy pig's nose, paint the cup pink and add two nostrils painted black
  - for an easy bunny nose, paint white or pink, add a pompom and pipe cleaners for whiskers, paint or draw on the mouth and whisker-freckles
  - for an easy frog nose, paint green with spots
- Let paint or glue dry completely.
- Wear like a very little mask.

More Ideas

Create other costume-like features from the egg carton such as ears and tails.

Attach lightweight circles cut from the egg carton to the nose cup to look like eyes. Decorate with art materials. Add eyebrows and eyelashes.

Attach a mustache to the nose.

Moving Eyes Mask

Create an intriguing device to see how eyes affect facial expressions.

Materials

heavy paper plate
scissors
old file folder
crayons or markers

Steps

- Cut 1″ (3 cm) slits at either side of the plate at eye level.
- Cut holes for the eyes.
- Draw a nose and mouth. Draw eyebrows too.
- Cut strips from the file folder, about 1″ x 20″ (3 cm x 60 cm).
- Slip a strip in one slit, behind the eye holes, and out the other strip.
- Draw two eyeballs in the eye holes on the strip.
- Pull the strip to one side until both eyes are blank again. Draw more eyes, different from the first set.
- Keep pulling and drawing different sets of eyes until the strip is filled with sets of eyes.
- Hold up the mask and pull the moving eyes strip for the enjoyment of others watching. The face will be animated by different eye expressions.

More Ideas

Think up imaginary things to say (dialogue) that go with the different eye expressions of the mask. Some examples:

for surprised eyes–"Oh, I think there's a spider in my shirt!"
for sleepy eyes–"I need my blanket and my pillow."
for happy eyes–"This puppy is the best present I have ever received!"

Cut an open mouth in the paper plate. Prepare a blank strip of paper to pull behind the mouth hole. Draw different mouths and teeth on a strip. Look through blank eye holes while pulling the mouth strip. Look in the mirror or ask someone to watch you.

Decorate the paper-plate moving mask with hair, beard, ears, hat, or any variety of noses.

Box Costume

THE BASE OF A GREAT COSTUME SUCH AS A CAR, AIRPLANE, FISH BOWL, OR ANIMAL IS A PLAIN CARDBOARD BOX. IMAGINATION DOES ALL THE REST.

Materials

grocery box big enough to climb into
scissors and other cutting tools (sharp ones for adult only)
stapler and tape
2 strips of strong, wide cloth about 2′ long (1 m) each to use for shoulder straps
crayons, paints, or markers

Steps

- Think about what the box costume will be the base for: an animal, car, airplane, rocket, fish bowl, etc. For this project, a horse shape will be used, but any shape of choice is fine.
- Draw the horse shape on the box.
- With adult help, cut away some of the box so the horse shape is left. Leave a hole in the top of the box for the child to poke his upper body through.
- Attach the strips of cloth for shoulder straps with the stapler and extra tape. Adjust the straps to fit the child.
- Paint or decorate the box to be a horse (or other idea).
- When dry, wear the box costume and enjoy pretending.

More Ideas

Cut a hole in the top of the box big enough for only the child's head to come through. The shoulders will hold the box at shoulder height.

Goofy Photo Opportunity

2 ★★

Create a backdrop, "ham it up," then take pictures of a goofy time. A few added props make the pretending even more fun!

Materials

camera and film
blank wall or old sheet
choices of materials to create the back drop, such as
fabric scraps and glue • masking tape • paints and brushes
paper scraps and glue • pushpins • scissors • props

Steps

- Decide on a scene or back drop to set up for the photo opportunity, such as
  circus or clowns • fairy glen • fantasy flowers • favorite sport • jungle • outer space
- Next, bring in a few props to extend the back drop, such as for a
  jungle—rubber snake, safari hat
  circus—clown suit, face paint, acrobat clothes, elephant trunk
  sport—football helmet and ball, tennis racket, skates
  fantasy flowers—scarf for butterfly wings, bumblebee antennae
  fairy glen—wings, wand, crown
  outer spaces—pace helmet
- Pose beside the scenery with the help of a prop or two.
- A second person takes a picture. What a goofy photo opportunity!

Note: If possible, use a Polaroid® or digital camera for instant results. Otherwise, have film developed as usual, but as quickly as possible.

More Ideas

Involve a favorite friend, relative, or pet in the set-up.
Make a scrapbook or photo album of favorite photographs.

I'm in the Bag

The possibilities are endless with this basic bag pattern. Create an apple, grape, balloon, tomato, ladybug, pumpkin, mouse, or anything else stuffed round with newspaper.

Materials

large piece of fabric, 2-3 yards (2-3 m)
NOTE: The color or pattern will change with each individual costume's theme.
stapler
needle and thread, optional
elastic or ribbon
scissors
accessories, collage items, or decorations (select a few)
aluminum foil • art tissue scraps • beads • bows • buttons • colored paper • corks
cotton balls • crepe paper • fabric scraps • feathers • felt scraps • glitter • hobby gems •
paper bag • pipe cleaners • pompoms • ribbons • sequins • sewing trims • yarn • zippers
shoes to accessorize the costume, optional
face paint or make-up to accessorize the costume, optional
newspaper, full crumpled sheets or shredded, to stuff the bag

Steps

- Measure a piece of fabric about as wide as from elbow to elbow, and double from chin to knee. Fold it in half, wrong side out. Staple the sides together, leaving holes for the arms. (Sew the sides together, if preferred.) Cut two holes in the fold for legs to poke through. Then turn right side out.
- To later cinch the bag at the neck, cut holes every 3″ to 6″ (8 cm to 15 cm). Run a piece of elastic or ribbon through these slits, in and out. Leave extra for tying.
- Decorate the costume to go with its theme, such as adding black dots for a lady bug. The following are suggestions only; come up with your own ideas!
  - apple–red fabric, green bow on head
  - ladybug–red fabric, black dots of paper, headband with pipe cleaner feelers
  - grape–purple or green fabric
  - tomato–red fabric, green hat
  - pumpkin or jack-o-lantern–orange fabric, black paper facial features, green hat
  - mouse–gray fabric, white tummy, ears on headband, long rope tail

Step into the bag. Stuff with newspaper until it is puffy and round. Cinch the bag comfortably around the neck and tie. Add additional accessories, such as shoes, hat, or make-up.

Two Poster Poses

3

I CAN BE ME,
I CAN BE YOU, I CAN BE ANYONE
I WANT TO BE WITH THESE TWO IDEAS
FOR PRETENDING.

Materials

heavy poster board
paints and brushes, optional
photocopy machine
scissors
tape
glue
markers
photograph of child
camera, optional

Steps

Idea one

- Cut an oval in the poster board to fit a full-size child's face (see illustration).
- Cut out the oval with scissors.
- Draw or paint the rest of the body on the poster in normal daily clothing, or decorate with imaginative make-believe clothing or costume. Let dry, if painted.
- Hang the poster from a doorway or clothesline with tape at child height so the child's face will line up with the oval.
- Stand behind the poster with the face placed into the oval. Smile, or make appropriate expressions to match the costume. (Note: Someone can take a picture if a camera is handy!)

Idea two

- Draw a real-size face oval on the poster board (or butcher paper).
- Draw the rest of the body around this oval, including hair and clothing. Clothing can be imaginary or real.
- From a photograph of the child's face, enlarge on a photocopy machine until it is normal facial size. (Note: a 3″ x 5″ or 8 cm x 12 cm full-face portrait picture would need to enlarge approximately 200%. This takes a little experimentation to get it right.)
- Cut out the oval part of the enlarged photocopied face and glue it to the oval.

More Ideas

Attach other photos or a drawn self-portrait.
Make a hand print or footprint on the poster.
Write or fill in personalized sentences or decorative additions to the poster, such as "My pets are _____ " • "My favorite thing to do is _______" • "My favorite dinner is _____".

Fabric-Mâché Mask

FABRIC-MÂCHÉ IS A UNIQUE LONG-LASTING ALTERNATIVE TO TRADITIONAL PAPIER-MÂCHÉ. CREATE A MASK THAT WILL LAST FOR YEARS TO COME. WEAR IT OR DISPLAY IT ON A SHELF FOR ALL TO SEE.

Materials

large cereal bowl, about 6″ x 3″ (15 cm x 8 cm)
newspaper
plasticine (plastic modeling clay, nonhardening type)
petroleum jelly
plastic wrap
white glue mixed with water in a medium bowl
strips of fabric scraps
paints and brush
additional decorative materials of choice, such as
buttons • feathers • glitter • yarn
clear acrylic spray (or any shiny hobby coating), optional (adult help needed)
sewing elastic, two pieces (heavy string also works)

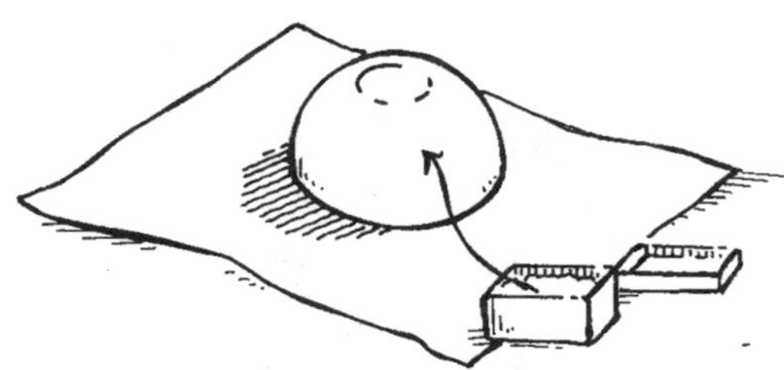

Steps

- Spread newspaper on a work surface. Turn the bowl upside down on the newspaper to act as the mold or form for the mask.
- Cover the bowl with plasticine (play clay that doesn't dry out). Form shapes and features with more plasticine.
- Cover the plasticine with petroleum jelly. This will keep the fabric strips from sticking later.
- Dip a strip of fabric in the glue mixed with water. Press into place over the mask. Dip another strip into the glue and place on the mask. Continue dipping and placing strips until the mask is covered. Create eye holes now, or cut them out later.
- Dry overnight until hard. Drying for several additional days will allow the mask to dry completely. When dry, carefully lift the mask away from the mold.
- Cut eye holes, if needed, then paint or decorate the mask.
- Glue on yarn, glitter, buttons, feathers, or any collage items on hand.
- For a shiny coating, spray in a well-ventilated area with clear acrylic spray paint or paint with any shiny hobby coating.
- To wear, punch holes with a pointed scissors or heavy duty hole punch in the sides on the same level as the eyes and ears. Insert a piece of stretch sewing elastic in each hole. Wear and enjoy! Or display on a shelf!

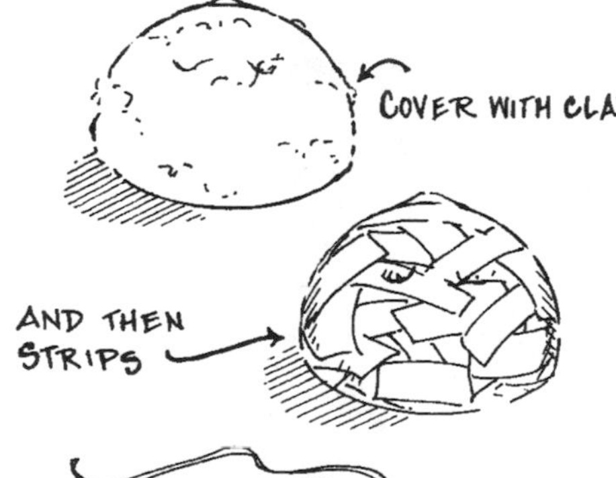

Storybook Play & Pretend

Chapter 5

★ 1

Daylight Pajama Party

DRESS UP IN COZY PAJAMAS, SNACK ON MILK AND COOKIES, SNUGGLE IN BLANKETS WITH PILLOWS, AND SAY GOODNIGHT TO EVERYTHING IN SIGHT, INCLUDING THE MOON AND MR. NOBODY. REMEMBER TO BRING A STUFFED ANIMAL TO HUG!

GOODNIGHT MOON BY MARGARET WISE BROWN, ILLUSTRATED BY CLEMENT HURD (NEW YORK: HARPERCOLLINS, 1947)

Materials

Goodnight Moon by Margaret Wise Brown
pajamas
blanket or sleeping bag, pillow
stuffed animal
bedtime snack idea: cookies and milk
optional props like those things found in the little bunny's room, such as
bedside lamp • dollhouse • mouse

Steps

- Read the bedtime book, *Goodnight Moon*. Notice all of the things the mother bunny in the rocking chair helps the little bunny say goodnight to in his great green room.
- After reading the book, set up a cozy pretend bed made of a blanket or sleeping bag and pillow. Bring a favorite stuffed toy. Keep it simple with just a few props or add many props.
- Wear pajamas and snuggle into the pretend bed. Have a bedtime snack.
- Say goodnight to everything in the room, just like the bunny in the story.
- Then pretend to go to sleep. Maybe take a real nap!

More Ideas

Bake sugar cookies that look like moons and stars.
Play with doll furniture set up like a bedroom, with a toy baby bunny in the bed, and a mama bunny in the rocking chair. Reenact the story through play. A flannel board is also a good way to reenact the story.
Read another Margaret Wise Brown bunny book, *The Runaway Bunny*.

Blanket Mitten

1 ★

THE MITTEN BY ALVIN TRESSELT, ILLUSTRATED BY YAROSLAVA MILLS (NEW YORK: LOTHROP, 1964)

BE READY FOR THE BUILD UP OF EXCITEMENT AND THE BOOM OF A BALLOON BURSTING—A VERY ROUSING MAKE-BELIEVE EXPERIENCE FOR ALL!

Materials

The Mitten by Alvin Tresselt or any other author
two blankets
big balloon
masks, optional

NOTE: PATTERNS FOR THE MASKS FOR THIS STORY CAN BE FOUND ON THE INTERNET AT http://www.janbrett.com. CHARACTERS ARE MOUSE, FROG, OWL, RABBIT, FOX, WOLF, BOAR, BEAR, CRICKET, AND A LITTLE BOY.

Steps

- Read *The Mitten* once through for enjoyment.
- The next time the story is read, set up two big blankets to form a mitten that children can crawl into, pretending to be the different animals in the story. As each animal crawls inside the mitten, blow up a big balloon a little at a time.
- When the story approaches the point where the mitten is filled with animals and about to pop, pop the balloon! The mitten can explode at the same time and all the animals (children) will come spilling out.
- To enhance make-believe, download mask patterns for this story from the Jan Brett website listed above. Or make masks from paper plates or other materials (see mask-making ideas in Chapter 4).
- Play "The Mitten" as a story participation activity while the story is read, or reenact the story from memory as a pretend activity following the reading.

More Ideas

Sew a big mitten shape from a yard of scrap fabric, or use an old pillowcase. Collect toy animals to play "The Mitten." Use the animals in the story or the ones on hand.

Act out the story while listening to a tape-recorded version.

Form a giant mitten with a tarp: staple together on one side, and Velcro the other side so it can easily burst open.

1 Curious George Play Corner

WITH A FEW PROPS FROM THE BOOK, CHILDREN RETELL AND REENACT GEORGE'S EXPERIENCES, AND THEN SOME FROM THEIR OWN IMAGINATIONS!

CURIOUS GEORGE BY H.A. REY (BOSTON: HOUGHTON MIFFLIN COMPANY, 1941)

Materials

Curious George by H.A. Rey
big straw hat
stuffed toy monkey (Curious George toy monkeys are available commercially)
toy telephone

Steps

- To begin, read the *Curious George* story about how George the monkey was captured in the jungle by the man with the yellow hat. Look at what George does with props in the story such as the telephone. Make a point of noting these.
- In a corner, set up a small desk or table and a telephone, then place the monkey and straw hat there too. Let the pretending and make-believe occur naturally with the dramatic stimulation of these props.
- Pretend to be George, the man with the yellow hat, make up and play new stories about George as a personal friend. Enact the actual story, or make up new ideas.

More Ideas

Read additional Curious George books in this wonderful series. Add props that encourage creative play and pretend based on these books. For example, for the book *Curious George Goes to the Hospital*, provide a jigsaw puzzle, pajamas for George, and a doctor's kit. For *Curious George Gets a Job*, provide newspapers, a delivery bag, a few rubber duckies, and a pretend bicycle made from a sawhorse.

Dress up like Curious George in various outfits from his different books. George is often seen wearing a yellow T-shirt.

Make a Curious George "story box" in a shoebox with the mini-props that he needs for some of his adventures.

Bridge Building

1

The Three Billy Goats Gruff written and illustrated by Paul Galdone (New York: Clarion, 1973)

This classic folktale is perfect for pretending with a few very simple props. This story will be acted and played again and again, with continuing enjoyment and enthusiasm!

Materials

The Three Billy Goats Gruff by Paul Galdone or any other author
props for the bridge, such as
- blocks—hollow play blocks lined up in a row make a noisy bridge
- masking tape—tape strips to a carpet to indicate the bridge
- chair or low stool—step up and onto a chair as the bridge; two children's short school chairs placed face to face are stable and the backs can be used like railings; drape a sheet over the chairs to make a little more of a hiding place for the troll
- low balance beam—pull into an open area to use as a bridge
- carpet sample scraps—line up on a bare floor to signify the bridge
- real bridge—go to a park or garden that has a real bridge

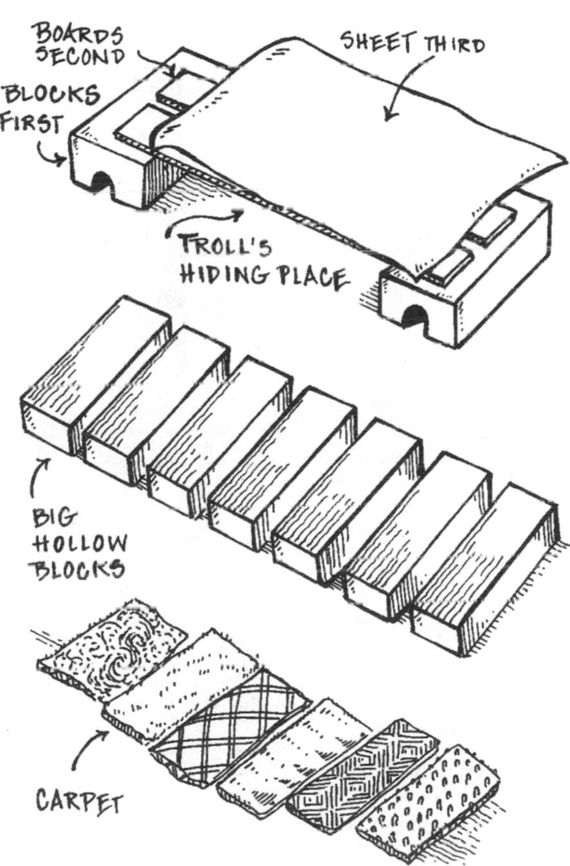

Steps

- Read the story aloud. Emphasize the words "Trip, Trap, Trip, Trap" and use dramatic voices for the different characters.
- Set up a bridge and reenact the story together. One side of the bridge is where the goats live, and the other side is the hill where they want to go. Use different voices for the three sizes of the goats, and of course, an especially gruff voice for the troll.
- Play "Three Billy Goats Gruff" following the story in the book, or adding imaginative new adventures for the goats and the troll and their troublesome bridge.

More Ideas

Place the following in the sand or sand table: three plastic goats, some wood scraps to build a bridge, and other tools for forming the hill.
Make characters for the flannel board for playing with the story.
Make stick puppets or other puppet ideas found in Chapter 3, pages 57-87.

1 Hospital Helpers

TRANSFORM A CORNER OF THE ROOM INTO A HOSPITAL, COMPLETE WITH MEDICAL PROPS, A BED, SPECIAL TOYS, AND PLAY GIFTS TO MAKE THE SICK PERSON FEEL MUCH BETTER. PRETEND TO BE MADELINE, OR ANYONE ELSE.

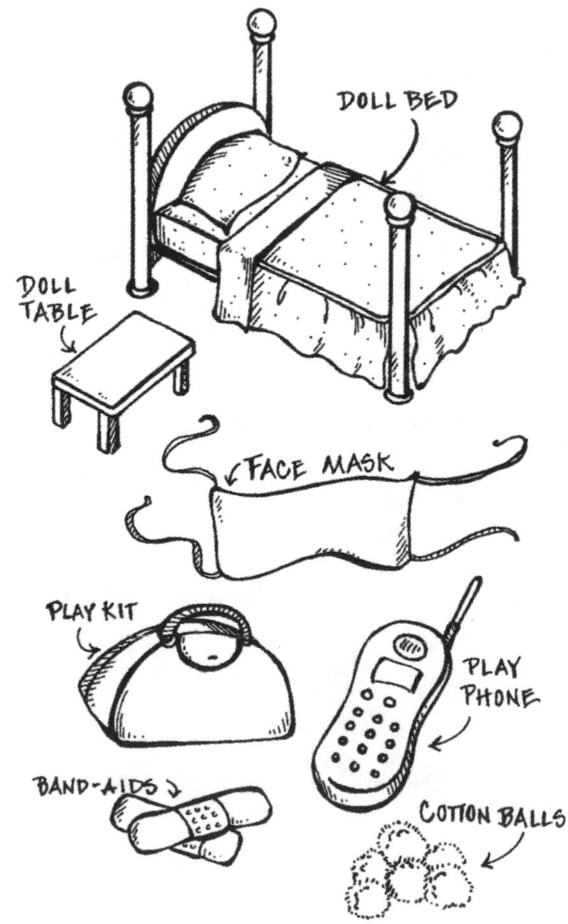

MADELINE BY LUDWIG BEMELMANS (NEW YORK: PUFFIN BOOKS, 1939)

Materials

Madeline by Ludwig Bemelmans
medical props, such as
bandages • Band-Aids • clipboard with paper • cotton balls • doctor's or nurse's kit
face mask or filter • hand lotion • medical clothing, lab coats • pads of paper
pencils • play syringe • stethoscope • tape measure • tongue depressors • weigh scale
hospital room props, such as
bedside table • blanket • pillow • play bed • telephone • wheel chair
hospital gifts and toys, such as
balloon • books • candy • cards • coloring book • comics • doll • flowers
greeting cards • magazines • puzzles • stuffed toy
materials to make get-well cards, optional
crayons, markers, pencils • envelopes • paper

Steps

- Read *Madeline* by Ludwig Bemelmans, about the little French girl who goes to the hospital to have her appendix out.
- Set up a play corner to resemble a hospital room. Start with a few simple props, then add others as needed. Keep in mind that some supplies can only be used once for health reasons, like tongue depressors.
- Put out materials for making get-well cards. Draw cards to help a "sick" friend feel better. Deliver them to the hospital. Bring other gifts as part of the play.
- When one person is better, she gets to have a turn to be the doctor or nurse, and another person can have a turn being ill.
- Pretend to be Madeline, or make up completely new stories, characters, and situations.

More Ideas

Read other Madeline books in this wonderful series.
Read *Curious George Goes to the Hospital* by H. A. Rey. Invite George to visit Madeline!

Sparkly Spider Web

Be Nice to Spiders by Margaret Bloy Graham (New York: HarperCollins, 1967)

"Be nice to spiders..." because they are beautiful, wondrous creatures who contribute positively to nature and the environment.

Materials

Be Nice to Spiders by Margaret Bloy Graham
silver or gold thread (elastic or plain)
square of matte board (from a frame shop), preferably black
scissors
suggested materials for the spider body
  acorn/nut • ball of foil • bead • cotton ball • gravel • pebble • wad of art tissue
suggested materials for spider legs
  pipe cleaners • string or cord • yarn pieces
art tools, such as
  glue, scissors, stapler, tape • paints and supplies • nail polish • paints and brushes
  white-out

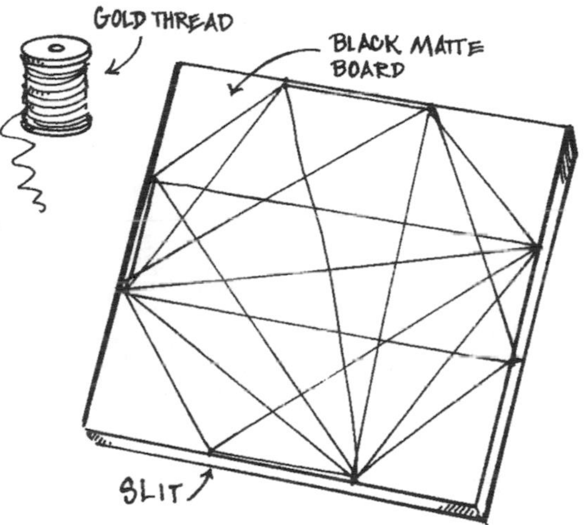

Steps

To make the web

- After reading *Be Nice to Spiders*, cut slits all around the edge of the matte board square. Cut no less than three and no more than ten. The slits need only be about ¼" to ½" (6 mm to 13 mm) long.
- Take a length of silver or gold thread and tuck the loose end into one of the slits. Now pull the thread across the board to another slit and pull in. Wrap to another slit, and then another, tucking the thread into the slit in the process. The thread will begin to weave a web crisscrossing the board. Weave back and forth, around and around, until the web is filled with threads any spider would be proud to own.
- Tuck the last end into a slit. Trim any extra thread.

To make the spider

- Construct a spider from one of the suggested materials listed on page 115. One of the easiest to use is a pebble. Paint the body, if desired, or leave plain.
- A spider has eight legs, so cut four pieces of yarn or other material. Lay the legs across the underside of the spider, sticking out on both sides to make eight legs. Cover with a heavy drop or puddle of glue to hold. Let the glue dry overnight. (A cool glue gun will work instantly, with adult help. Another alternative is to use a piece of tape to hold the legs in place.)

To put the spider and web together

- Place the spider on the web. Tuck it into the threads so it will hold.
- Play and pretend that the spider is weaving his web and catching food in the web.
- Undo the web at any time, and reweave in patterns as desired.
- Display the web on the wall or in the garden.

I'm a Storyteller!

THE SNOWMAN BY RAYMOND BRIGGS (NEW YORK: RANDOM HOUSE, 1978)

SET UP A PLAY LIBRARY CORNER FOR READING AND CHECKING OUT BOOKS. THEN BECOME THE GUEST STORYTELLER FOR ANYONE WHO WOULD ENJOY ATTENDING A LIBRARY STORYTELLING EVENT—TOYS, PETS, OR PEOPLE.

Materials

The Snowman by Raymond Briggs
props for a pretend library, such as
  books on display • check-out desk • check-out materials, like a date stamp, ink pad, cards dolls, toys, pets, or people • many books in a shelf • pillows, rug, chairs • storyteller's chair of honor • poster announcing the storytelling event
materials to make and display a poster, such as
  crayons • large sheet of paper • markers • paints and brushes • pushpins • stapler • stickers • tape

Steps

- This haunting, imaginative, and wordless book, *The Snowman*, is about a little boy who flies over the world with his magical, kind, and gentle snowman friend. Read, look at, and enjoy the book a few times.
- Set up a library play corner with pillows, rugs, and chairs for reading; books to browse or read; a check-out desk with check-out materials; and a storyteller's chair of honor.
- Make a poster on a large sheet of paper that highlights the guest storytelling event. In particular, include a picture showing what story is going to be told. In this case, the book is *The Snowman*, but it could be any book or story. Display the poster.
- Invite people, pets, or toys to attend the storytelling event.
- Sit in the storyteller's chair of honor and tell the story of the snowman and the little boy, making up the words in any way that suits the storyteller. Hold the book up to show pictures, or tell the story from the imagination.

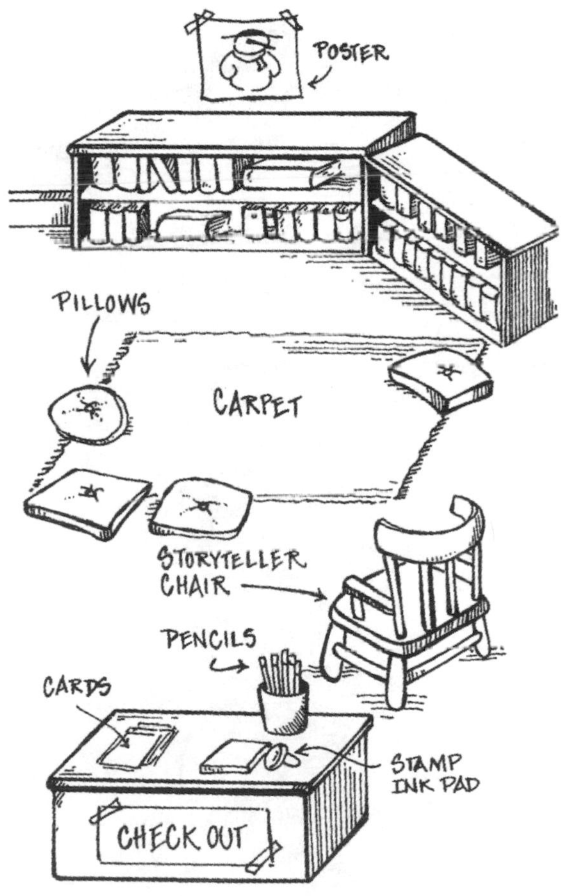

2 # Dyed Caps

MAKE COLORFUL CAPS FROM DYED PAINTER'S HATS, THEN REENACT THE STORY AS WRITTEN, OR "PLAY MONKEY SEE, MONKEY DO" PRETENDING TO BE A CLEVER PEDDLER WHO INVITES THE MONKEYS TO MIMIC HIM.

CAPS FOR SALE BY ESPHYR SLOBODKINA (NEW YORK: HARPERCOLLINS, 1940)

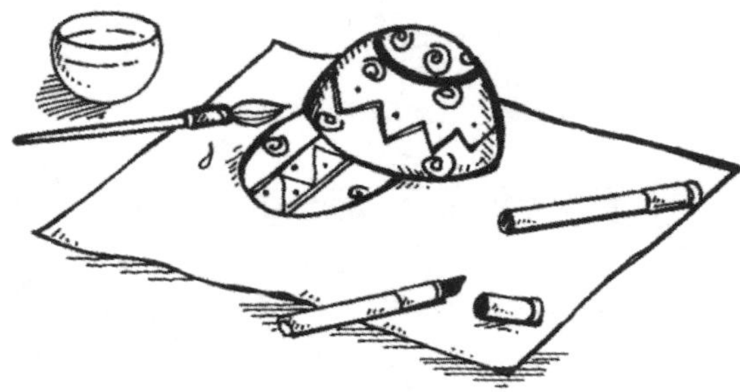

Materials

Caps for Sale by Esphyr Slobodkina
stack of painter's hats (ask for a free donation at a local paint or hardware store)
covered work area
permanent markers
alternate idea: Liquid Watercolor paints, brushes, and cups; spray-bottle

Steps

- Read *Caps for Sale* aloud, enjoying the mimicry of the monkeys.
- To make caps, spread the painter's hats out on a covered work area.
- Use permanent markers, Liquid Watercolors, or both. If using permanent markers only, begin drawing shapes and designs all over the hats to make them colorful. For Liquid Watercolors, pour colors into separate cups. Dip a paintbrush into the cups and paint directly on the hats. Fill hand spray bottles with Liquid Watercolor and spray on colors. Dry completely before wearing. When dry, use permanent markers for further decorating.
- When the caps are dry, pretend to be the peddler and stack them up tall on one person's head. When the peddler is sleeping, each monkey can steal a cap to wear.
- To play "Monkey See, Monkey Do," the peddler does actions and antics the monkeys can copy. (Monkeys can also do things that the peddler can copy!)

More Ideas

Make a monkey snack of banana chips and M&M's, banana bread, or banana muffins.
Enjoy chanting the rhyme "Five Little Monkeys Jumping on the Bed."

Five little monkeys jumping on a bed
One fell off and broke his head
Mama called the doctor and the doctor said,
"No more monkeys jumping on the bed!"
Then, Four little monkeys, next, three, then two, one, and finally, "No little monkeys jumping on the bed, They can't fall off and break their heads," etc.

Dancing Scarves

COLOR DANCE BY ANN JONAS (NEW YORK: GREENWILLOW BOOKS, 1989)

DYE WIDE STRIPS OF OLD SHEETS FOR COLORFUL AND EXCITING DANCING INDOORS OR OUT.

Materials

Color Dance by Ann Jonas
old sheet or other lightweight fabric
rubber gloves, optional
scissors
clothesline or drying rack
small buckets of warm water
open area for dancing
outdoor area for dyeing (and dancing!)
music, CD's or tapes
Liquid Watercolors in red, yellow, and blue (or food coloring)

Steps

- Read the book *Color Dance* by Ann Jonas, seeing how the colored scarves mix and blend their colors making new colors.
- Tear an old sheet into big wide strips, enough for at least three strips or one for each child interested in the dance. Snip the edge of the fabric with scissors to get the tearing started if needed. Any lightweight fabric will do, the lighter the better for dancing scarves that blow and billow.
- Working outside, place three buckets of warm water on the ground. Two cups of water per bucket is good for a start. More can always be added.
- Next add a big squirt of red Liquid Watercolor paint to the first bucket, yellow to the second, and blue to the third. If you wish, use food coloring.
- Push a torn strip down into each bucket and let soak briefly. Mix and squeeze the strip in the color until nicely colored. Then wring out over the bucket, squeezing excess color from the strips.

NOTE: WEAR GLOVES IF YOU WANT UNSTAINED HANDS, ALTHOUGH LIQUID WATERCOLOR WILL WASH OUT OVER THE SPAN OF A FEW DAYS.

- Dye as many strips as desired, adding more water and color as needed.
- Hang the strips to dry for several hours or overnight. Meanwhile, clean up the dye buckets.
- When the strips are dry, dance to music outdoors or in a large open indoor area, letting the wind blow the strips of color.

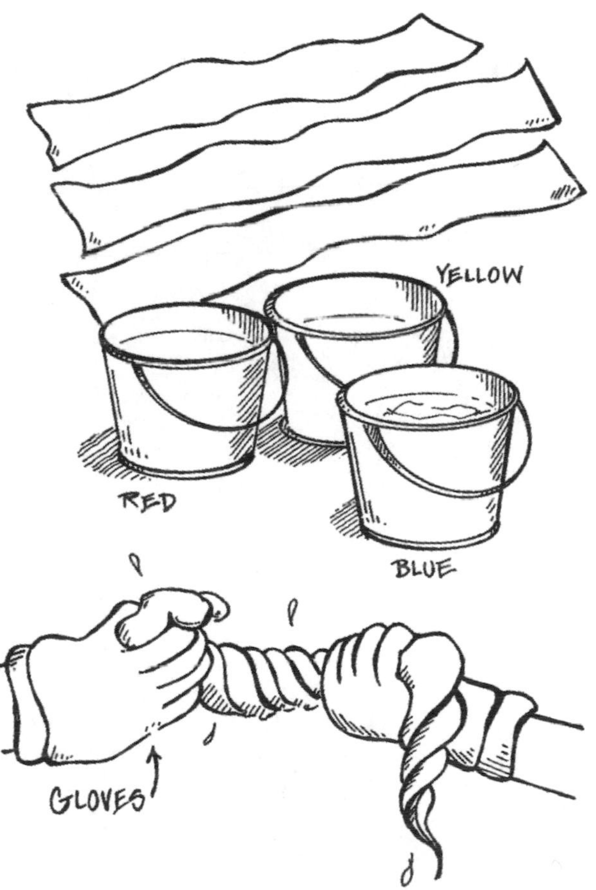

2

Purple Mural

JUST LIKE HAROLD, DRAW AN ADVENTURE WITH A PURPLE CRAYON, BUT IN THIS CASE, ON BIG, WHITE BUTCHER PAPER TAPED TO A PLAIN WALL

HAROLD AND THE PURPLE CRAYON BY CROCKETT JOHNSON (NEW YORK: HARPERCOLLINS, 1955)

Materials

Harold and the Purple Crayon by Crockett Johnson
purple crayon
large, white butcher or craft paper
plain wall
scissors
masking tape, stapler, or pushpins

Steps

- Read *Harold and the Purple Crayon* for enjoyment.
- To further explore Harold's magical world, first find a wide, empty expanse of wall without windows or doors.
- Hang the large paper on the wall, with the lower edge touching the floor and upper edge extending to a child's height. Two pieces of paper may be needed to reach as tall as a child can reach so she can stretch and draw just like Harold with his purple crayon.
- Draw a purple adventure on the big white paper on the wall. Draw all the details as they develop in the imagination. Fill the paper!

More Ideas

Work together with a friend on 8 ½″ x 11″ (20 cm x 28 cm) paper, talking through the sketches as they occur, helping each other draw solutions to problems, or sketching extensions to thrilling moments.

On a dry erase board or a chalkboard, draw an adventure with a purple pen or purple chalk.

Paint or color the mural when done.

Mix red and blue paints to make purple. Paint an all purple painting in different shades of purple.

Thumbkin Tiny Tea

Miss Spider's Tea Party by David Kirk, Antoinette White (New York: Scholastic, 1994)

Enjoy a lovely miniature tea party with a tea set made from polymer clay and each cup or accessory fashioned over the thumb—just the right size for Miss Spider or other doll friends.

Materials

Miss Spider's Tea Party by David Kirk
polymer clay, such as Sculpey III or Fimo
thumb
cornstarch to 1″ (3 cm) deep in a small dish
other accessories, such as
- bandanna or other fabric square for picnic cloth
- large flat buttons for plates
- scraps of fabric or paper towel for napkins

tools to help sculpt, such as
- bamboo skewers • plastic knife • spatula

toothpicks
glass baking pan recommended
oven preheated according to manufacturer's directions

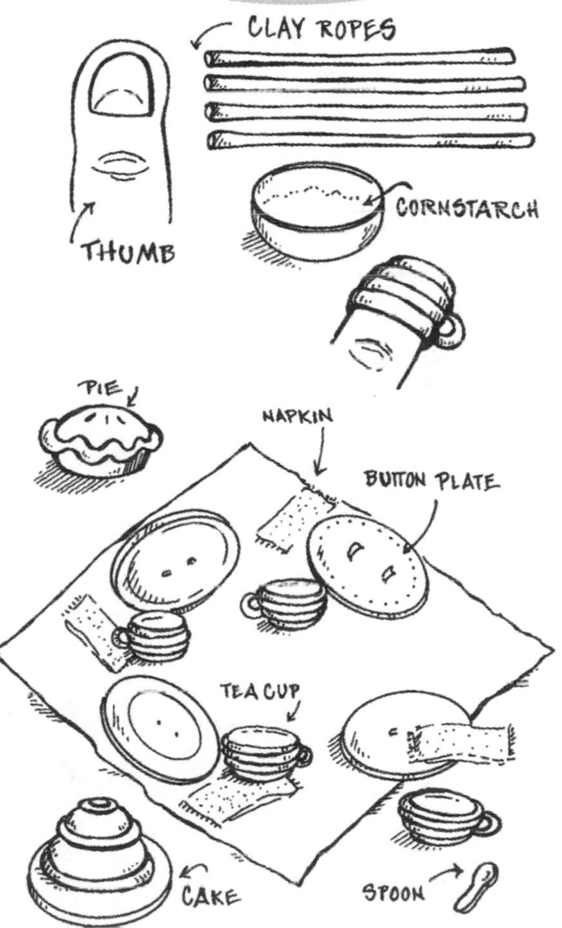

Steps

- First read the story of *Miss Spider's Tea Party* for enjoyment.
- To make the tea settings for a pretend tea party, roll clay into long ropes ¼″ to ½″ (.5 cm to 1 cm) thick. Roll several to have ready ahead of time.
- Next, dip a thumb on the nonworking hand in the cornstarch. (If right handed, dip the left thumb.) This will help the clay slip from the thumb more easily. To make a cup for the tea party, coil a rope of clay around the thumb (see illustration). Three to four coils should be enough.
- Remove the clay, cutting away the extra coil. Shape the cup further as desired, flattening the bottom if you like. Use the extra coil to make a little cup handle. Press to stick with a toothpick or bamboo skewer. Then place on the glass baking pan.

- Continue making cups. Four is a nice even number for a tea party, but the choice is up to the party giver! Place on the baking pan with the others.
- To make a sugar bowl or creamer, start with the basic coiled cup shape, and then make two handles for the sugar bowl, and a pinched edge for the creamer. Make a lid for the sugar bowl from a flat piece of clay with a little loop or ball on the top, attached and pressed on with a toothpick or skewer. Place these on the baking pan with the other pieces.
- Bake according to the recommendations on the clay package. Let cool before removing.
- While the clay is cooling, spread out the picnic tablecloth. Make the napkins from scraps of fabric or pieces of paper towel. Set the table with big flat buttons for plates. Make sure everything is ready!
- Now add the cooled tea set pieces, and have a lovely pretend tea party. Make believe you are Miss Spider, or think up a tea party for dolls or other toys.

More Ideas

Sculpt little cakes, cookies, or pies with the clay. Bake right along with the cups. Serve at the tea party for festive pretend delights.

Instead of coiling the clay, sculpt a tea party set in any fashion.

Hungry Sock Puppet

The Very Hungry Caterpillar by Eric Carle (New York: Philomel Books, 1969)

To play make-believe as a very very hungry caterpillar, construct a sock puppet with an endlessly empty tummy who can eat plastic fruits and any number of other things whole.

Materials

old big sock, stocking hat, or a long sleeve from an old T-shirt or sweatshirt
items to decorate the caterpillar, such as
beads • buttons • felt scraps • googly craft eyes • paper scraps • stickers
oatmeal cylinder box (small to medium), or a potato chip can

tape	stapler
scissors	*The Very Hungry Caterpillar* by Eric Carle
glue	plastic or toy fruit (pretend fruit can be made from cardboard cutouts)

Steps

- Read *The Very Hungry Caterpillar* by Eric Carle for enjoyment.
- To make a hungry caterpillar puppet, pull off the top of the box and put it in the scrap box. With adult help, cut a big mouth hole in the oatmeal box as shown in the illustration. Turn the box upside down and the mouth will be about 2/3 of the way down the cylinder.
- Cut the big sock or stocking hat so that it becomes an open tube. Staple the sock or hat to the open circle end of the box. Some tape may also help attach the sock securely.

Optional Idea: If the sock or hat is large enough, pull it all the way over the cylinder box, like a foot in a sock. Then cut a hole in the sock to match right over the hole in the box. Tape edges together.

- Slip the arm up through the sock and into the box. The fingers of the hand can poke through the hole to act like hungry caterpillar teeth. This is where the "food" will go in.
- Decorate and cover the box and sock with whatever materials are on hand. Let any glue dry.

Note: If the sock was pulled over the box, no additional decoration is necessary, other than some eyes, spots, or antennae.

- Pull the hungry caterpillar puppet over one hand again. Now begin to retell the story, feeding the caterpillar whatever it must eat for each day of the week. The food will be grasped by the caterpillar's fingery teeth and pulled through the hole in the box-mouth, pushing down into the sock tube until the story's end.

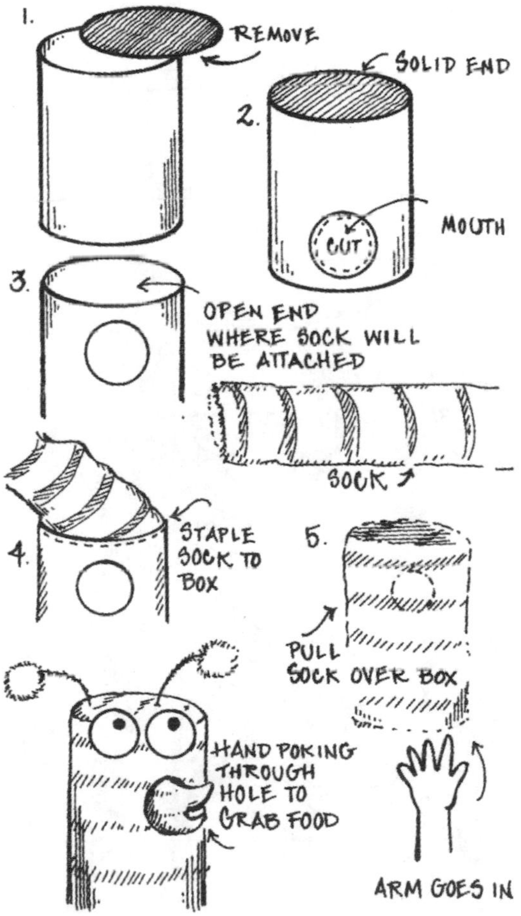

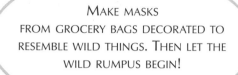

Wild Rumpus Masks

Make masks from grocery bags decorated to resemble wild things. Then let the wild rumpus begin!

Where the Wild Things Are by Maurice Sendak (New York: HarperCollins, 1963)

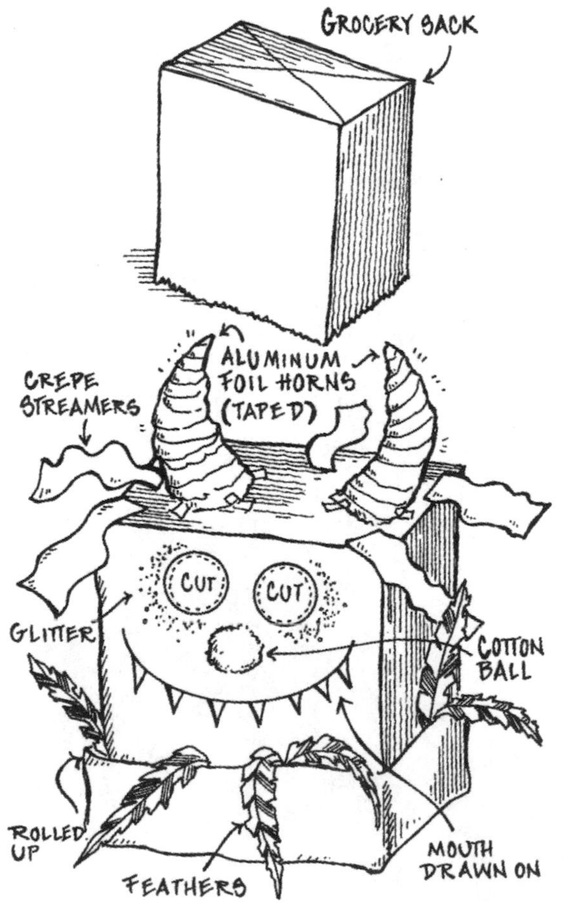

Materials

Where the Wild Things Are by Maurice Sendak
full-size paper grocery sacks
craft tools, such as
  glue • scissors • staplers • tape
coloring tools, such as
  brushes • crayons • markers • paints
collage and decorating suggestions
  aluminum foil • buttons • cellophane • colored paper scraps • cotton balls
  crepe paper streamers • egg cartons • feathers • felt pieces • glitter and sequins
  ribbons • sewing scraps • sewing trims • shredded paper • yarn

Steps

- Read *Where the Wild Things Are*, paying particular attention to the wild rumpus.
- To make grocery sack masks that look like "wild things," begin by pulling the paper sack over the head. Roll the sack's edge up to the shoulders, so the sack sits comfortably on the head.
- Feel where the eyes are under the mask. Gently and carefully make a dot on the sack over each eye's location. Then remove the sack. Cut holes for the eyes. Holes for a nose or mouth may also be cut at this time, or may be simply decorated onto the sack without holes.
- Use imagination to create a wild thing mask. It does not have to look like any of the wild things in the book, but the book may give some inspiration for features like horns, sharp teeth, big ears, and whiskers. Cut and paste, draw, paint, or otherwise attach things to the mask to make a wild thing. Try it on now and then to see how it's going.
- When done, put on the wild thing mask and have a wild rumpus just like Max.

More Ideas

Play a music game as part of the wild rumpus. When the music plays, everyone growls and stomps about. When the music stops, the rumpus stops too.

Sponge-Printed Snake

2

CRICTOR BY TOMI UNGERER (NEW YORK: HARPERCOLLINS, 1958)

CONSTRUCT A FULL-SIZED BOA CONSTRICTOR FROM AN OLD SHEET ROLLED INTO A SNAKE AND PAINTED WITH LIQUID WATERCOLOR PATTERNS OF LETTERS, NUMBERS, OR NEW SHAPES AND DESIGNS.

Materials

Crictor by Tomi Ungerer
old sheet
sponge pieces
newspapers
permanent marker
string, cut in 1′ (30 cm) lengths
scissors
tempera paint, Liquid Watercolors in cups, or fabric dye or food or food coloring

Steps

- Read *Crictor,* a story about a snake who can form letter shapes with his body.
- To make a snake shape, spread out the old sheet. Start at one corner and begin rolling the sheet towards the center. Keep on rolling until all that is left is the other corner. Take a piece of string and tie it around the center of the snake. Tie a knot. Cut off extra string.
- Tie another piece of string around the "head." Cut off extra string. Tie another around the tail, following the same directions. Tie pieces of string all along the snake about every 6″ to 12″ (15 cm to 30 cm), snipping extra string away.
- When the snake is tied in sections, spread its body out on newspapers.
- Dip a piece of sponge into Liquid Watercolor (or other source of color) and press on the snake's body. Make spots, patches, or other patterns. Fill the snake's body with colorful sponge prints. Use a permanent marker to give the snake some eyes and a mouth. Dry overnight (or place inside an old pillowcase and then in a dryer for 30 minutes or so). Now Crictor is ready for letter play.
- Wind and twist Crictor into letter shapes. Other shapes or numerals are fun for Crictor to work on too. Help Crictor learn about letters.

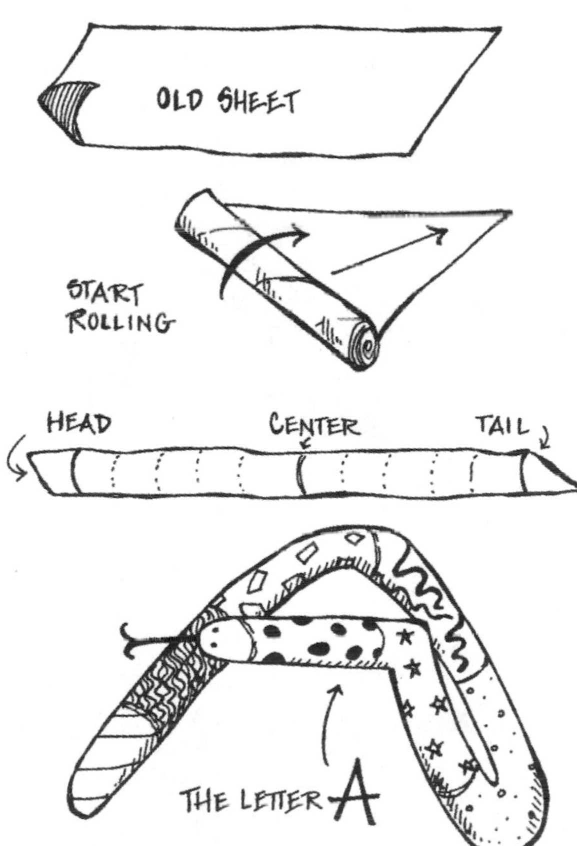

More Ideas

Sew on buttons for eyes, or glue on googly craft eyes.
Sew on a piece of red felt for a tongue for Crictor.
Make small clay Crictor's for writing words, letters, spelling names, and playing with other shapes and designs Crictor can make with his snakey body.

Postcards and Stamps

MAKE TASTY LICKABLE STAMP GLUE FOR STAMPS AND POSTCARDS. THEN PRETEND TO BE THE LETTER CARRIER WHO DELIVERS THEM.

NEVER MAIL AN ELEPHANT BY MIKE THALER, ILLUSTRATED BY JERRY SMATH
(MAHWAH, NJ: TROLL ASSOCIATES, 1993)

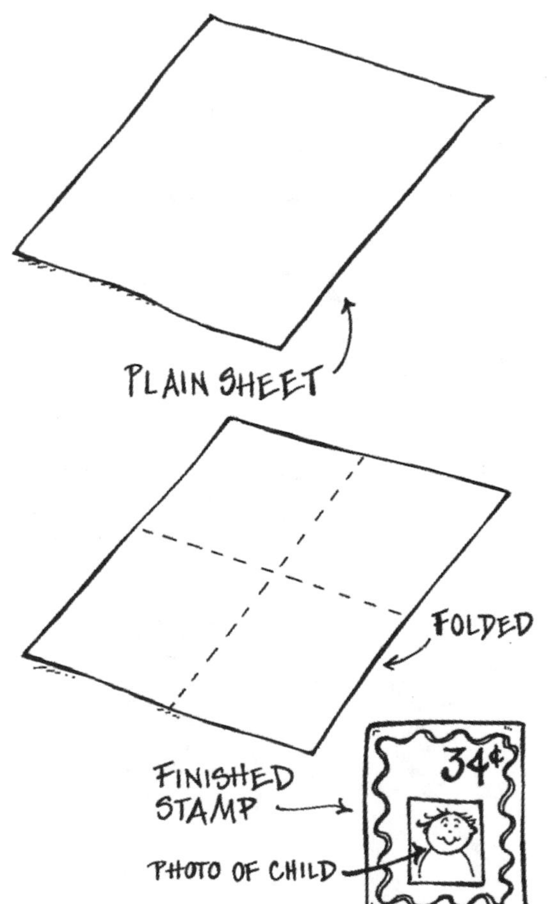

Materials

Never Mail an Elephant by Mike Thaler
plain white paper
materials for stamp glue
- 1 package unflavored gelatin
- 2 tablespoons of any fruit juice
- saucepan • brush

ruler
child-designed sheet of stamps
paper for postcards, such as
- heavy paper • old greeting cards • wrapping paper • magazine clippings
- photos • index cards

writing and drawing tools, such as
- colored pencils • crayons • markers • pens

scissors
glue, tape, paste
materials for dress-up play, optional
letter carrier hat (any suitable dress-up hat)
letter carrier shoulder delivery bag (old purse)

Steps

- Read the book *Never Mail an Elephant* by Mike Thaler about the process of preparing and sending mail in a delightfully funny way. The narrator has trouble mailing an elephant as a birthday present to Cousin Edna.
- First make a sheet of pretend stamps. Fold a piece of plain white paper into squares. Any size is fine, stamp size or larger. Draw or color a picture in each box. For most authentic stamps, write a number on the stamp that tells how much it is worth. Set aside until the stamp glue is ready.
- Make the glue for lickable stamps. Mix the gelatin and fruit juice in a small saucepan and heat. When cool, brush the glue on the back of a sheet of paper designed as stamps. Let dry. Cut the stamps apart on the folded lines. Set aside until the postcards are ready.
- Prepare postcards to pretend-mail. Use any heavy paper cut into card shapes, or use index cards. Decorate one side of the postcard with drawings, magazine clippings, photographs, wrapping paper, or other ideas. Then turn the card over. Write a message and also the name of the person to whom it is being mailed. Lick and stick on a stamp.
- Place the card in a pretend delivery bag, and deliver to the person for whom it is intended.

Millions of Dough Cats

2 ★★

Millions of Cats by Wanda Gag (New York: Putnam, 1928)

Little dough cats are created from a basic art clay recipe, and used to re-enact this classic story

Materials

copy of *Millions of Cats* by Wanda Gag (pronounced Van'dah Gog)
playdough, or for more permanent cat sculptures, make Basic Art Clay (recipe below)
paint and brushes, optional
wood blocks for hills, houses, paths
materials for the hills, such as scarves, fabric napkins
two small dolls or toy figures to resemble the old man and old woman

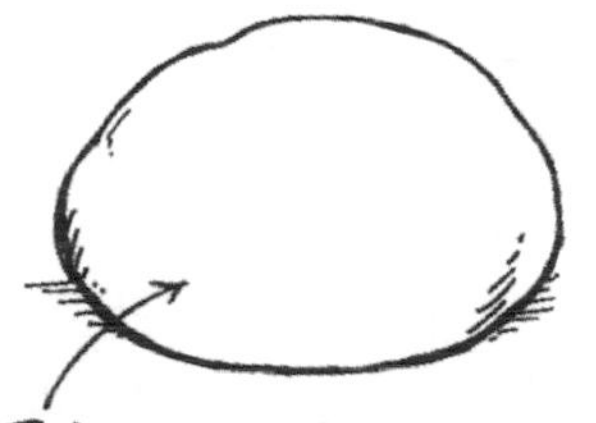

Steps

- Read the classic children's story *Millions of Cats*. Enjoy chanting, "Hundreds of cats, Thousands of Cats, Millions and Billions and Trillions of Cats."
- Make cats from the Basic Art Clay. A simple, featureless ball will be fine. Make as many as possible, but at least make ten!

Note: As an alternative idea, divide the dough into four or more balls. Color each ball of dough with food coloring so that the cats can be different colors. The easiest and longest-lasting cats are formed from one ball of clay, squeezed into shape, with ears pulled from the clay (not added on).

- Bake or air dry until hard. Cats may be painted when dry, if desired.
- Make a play scene of hills, paths, and a house with blocks and scarves. Draping the scarves over several stacked blocks makes the blocks look like hills. Line up blocks to form paths, and use blocks to build a house for the man and woman and the little kitten.
- Reenact the story, chanting the "Hundreds of cats..." words from the book while playing.

Basic Art Clay Recipe

Mix 4 cups (1 L) flour, 1 cup (240 ml) salt, and 1½ cups (360 ml) warm water in a bowl. Knead for ten minutes, or until soft and elastic. Model as with any clay or dough. For permanent sculptures, bake at 300°F (150°C) until hard. May be air dried instead, for a few days.

★★ 2

Traffic Course

WITH THIS BOOK AS INSPIRATION, SET UP A TRAFFIC COURSE FOR RIDING TOYS, WITH TRAFFIC SIGNS. PREPARE A FESTIVE PARADE WITH DECORATED VEHICLES ON THE MAIN STREET OF THE TRAFFIC COURSE!

CARS AND TRUCKS AND THINGS THAT GO BY RICHARD SCARRY (NEW YORK: GOLDEN PRESS, 1974)

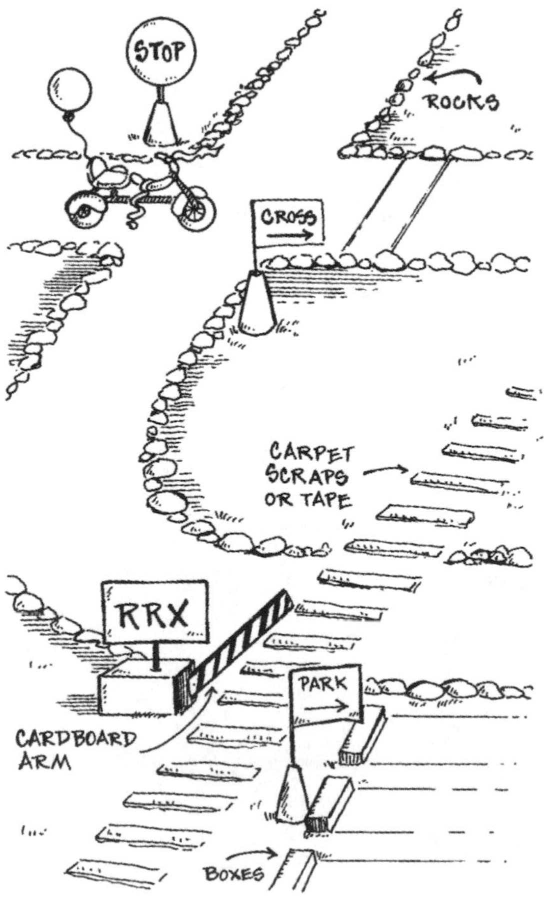

Materials

Cars and Trucks and Things That Go by Richard Scarry
riding toys
playground or indoor gym
roads and streets, made from
carpet sample scraps • chalk lines • masking tape • ropes • string • washable paint
traffic signs, made from
cardboard boxes • chairs • coat racks • crayons • heavy paper or newsprint
paint easels, paints, brushes
traffic cones
wide markers
materials to decorate riding toys, such as
clothespins • crepe paper • fabric scraps • flags • newspaper • paints, brushes
ribbons • sewing trim • stapler • streamers • tape • yarn
broom, dustpan

Steps

- Read about cars and trucks for enjoyment, noting the many kinds of vehicles Richard Scarry includes in this book.
- Build an obstacle or traffic course on a playground or a large indoor area. Sweep the area clean of rocks, glass, or debris.
- Spread out and arrange materials to indicate roads, paths, or streets from the list above. Have cross streets, one way streets, and speedways.
- Next put up signs made from boxes, posted on chairs or easels, or sticking on traffic cones. Begin with two or three signs and add others as needed. Signs to make are
  BRIDGE AHEAD • CARPOOL LANE • DO NOT ENTER • EXIT ONLY • GAS AHEAD
  LEFT TURN ONLY • ONE WAY • PARK • SPEED LIMIT 30 MPH • STOP • YIELD
- Drive riding toys through the traffic plan, paying attention to signs and rules.
- As a culmination, decorate the vehicles and have a parade through the course, with all traffic except the main street blocked off, of course. Play parade music, if desired.

Let's Have a Picnic

2 ★★

Teddy Bears' Picnic by Jimmy Kennedy, illustrated by Alexandra Day
(San Diego: Green Tiger Press, 1983)

Why not have a real picnic, just like the teddy bears? Pack baskets with snacks or lunch and picnic supplies, and bring play equipment for all of the games and fun. Don't forget to invite a favorite teddy bear!

Materials

Teddy Bears' Picnic by Jimmy Kennedy
picnic basket or cooler chest
ice in plastic bags
tablecloth and napkins
plates, cups, silverware
blanket to sit on
choice of good things to eat, such as
 apple juice • chocolate chip cookies • corn on the cob • cupcakes • fried chicken
 fruit salad • lemonade • peanut butter and jelly and/or tuna salad sandwiches
 potato salad
entertainment, games and sports equipment, such as
 balloons • balls • bubbles • hula hoops • kites • nerf balls
 plastic wicky-tape, to mark start and finish for races • ring toss • squirt guns
music on tape or CD, optional

Steps

- Begin by reading *Teddy Bears' Picnic* by Jimmy Kennedy about teddy bears who have a wonderful picnic.
- To prepare a real picnic, start by making food together. Pack the food into a basket or a cooler chest. Add ice in plastic bags to keep things cool.
- Pack up the toys for picnic fun. Don't forget to bring a favorite teddy bear!
- Head out to a park, to the playground, or to the back yard for a real picnic.
- Spread a blanket on the ground. If there is a picnic table, spread the tablecloth on the table. Set the table with silverware, plates, and cups for a picnic like the one in the book.
- Eat and enjoy! The teddy bears will surely want some bites, too.
- After cleaning up, it's time for games, races, music, balloons, and bubbles. Have a grand time!

More Ideas

Have an indoor picnic on the floor on a rainy day. Invite all the teddy bears to dress up in doll clothes and attend the festivities.

Bus Scene

Draw a wall scene to look like a bus with windows, then set up the seats and enjoy playing bus driver, bus, and passengers.

The Wheels on the Bus: An adaptation of the original song by Maryann Kovalski (Boston: Little, Brown, and Company, 1987)

Materials

The Wheels on the Bus by Maryann Kovalski
large sheet of butcher or craft paper to make the bus mural
bus props, such as
baby car seat • chairs, blocks, or boxes to sit on • dolls or toys as passengers
newspaper, magazines, books • plastic jar for collecting fares • poker chips for play money
real steering wheels • shopping bag, backpack, package
markers, crayons, or pencils to draw passing scenes in the windows of the bus
tape, stapler, or pushpins to hang mural at child height, just off the floor
scissors
song "The Wheels on the Bus" (some of the verses included on page 131)

Steps

- Read *The Wheels on the Bus*, and sing the song too!
- Design the bus wall scenery on a large piece of butcher paper but in a bus shape. Don't forget the wheels!
- Draw big rectangles to indicate windows. In each window, draw a scene that someone might see if looking out the bus windows. Each window can have a different scene, such as might be seen in real life, or completely imaginary or fantasy.
- Attach the bus mural to the wall with the wheels just touching the floor.
- Just beside the bus, set up the "seats" made of chairs, boxes, or blocks to sit on. Try to have at least four seats, but no more than ten. Give the driver a special seat.
- Now play bus! The driver collects fares, passengers come and go whenever they reach their stops. Everyone sings "The Wheels on the Bus"!

When singing the "Wheels on the Bus" song, make up original verses about the different passengers, bus parts, and the driver, and what they might say or sound like. Here are some of the words and verses along with new ones children have added:

The wheels on the bus go round and round, round and round, round and round.
(roll hands one over the other)
The wheels on the bus go round and round
All through the town.

The people on the bus go bump, bump, bump; bump, bump, bump; bump, bump, bump.
(move up and down)
The people on the bus go bump, bump, bump
All through the town.

The wipers on the bus go swish, swish, swish; swish, swish, swish; swish, swish, swish.
(move arm back and forth)
The wipers on the bus go swish, swish, swish
All through the town.

The babies on the bus go wah, wah, wah...
(pretend to cry)

The driver on the bus says move on back...
(move arm over shoulder)

The mothers on the bus go mwah, mwah, mwah...
(make kissing sounds)

...and so on and so on
All through the town!

More Ideas

Play taxi, train, airplane, or other mode of transportation.

Add dress-up clothes to the pretend scene, such as hats or outfits that people on the bus might wear. Some characters might be a construction worker • sailor • baby • cowboy • nurse • astronaut • dancer • waiter • baker

3 ! Three Box Houses: Easy Play Scenery

CONSTRUCT THREE HOUSES FROM LARGE APPLIANCE BOXES DESIGNED TO RESEMBLE THE CUSTOMARY HOUSES OF STRAW, STICKS, AND BRICK. CONSIDER PUTTING ON A LEISURELY PLAY FOR FAMILY OR FRIENDS.

THE THREE LITTLE PIGS BY PAUL GALDONE (NEW YORK: HOUGHTON MIFFLIN, 1979)

Materials

The Three Little Pigs by Paul Galdone, or any other version of this story
3 large cardboard appliance boxes
knife to cut cardboard (adult managed/directed by child)
tempera paints in cups, and brushes
newspapers to cover floor

Steps

- First read the story for enjoyment. When the story is familiar, find three heavy duty cardboard appliance boxes such as dishwashers or refrigerators come in.
- Cut the boxes with a sharp knife to allow for a hinged door, windows, chimneys, and so on. The adult handles the knife while following the child's design. Complete all three boxes to resemble houses of straw, sticks, and bricks.
- Spread newspapers under each house. Paint the boxes as straw, sticks, and bricks. Add other painted decoration to the brick house such as doorknob, flower pot, bushes, window shade, or curtains. When satisfied with the painting, allow to dry completely.
- When dry, remove the newspapers and set up the boxes for playing the three pigs and wolf. Switch parts so everyone can be the wolf or the smartest pig.
- When comfortable with the free play and pretend, invite others to watch an informal presentation.

More Ideas

Costumes are not necessary, but here are some suggestions for simple ones:

Make a cardboard headband and staple paper ears to it for pigs or wolf; tape tales to the waistband of pants or skirts.

Make noses from the cardboard cups of an egg carton; with paint or markers, draw pig noses or a wolf nose. (See page 102).

Make a simple mask that is held up in front of the face by drawing on a paper plate and then stapling it to a tongue depressor.

Find simple dress-up clothes such as coveralls, hats, or work clothes for the characters to wear.

Three Bears Story Box

GLUE 3

Goldilocks and the Three Bears retold and illustrated by Jan Brett
(New York: Dodd, Mead & Company, 1987)

Construct a story box with the characters of the three bears and Goldilocks, all snuggled into one little cigar box, set up for enduring play and pretend, time after time.

Materials

Goldilocks and the Three Bears by Jan Brett
empty cigar box or school supply box with lid (shoebox will also work fine)
materials to make bears, such as
- 3 plastic bears (cake decorating supplies are a good source)
- 3 small bear toys
- or make your own bears with 3 empty sewing spools glued with felt scraps for ears and clothes, permanent markers for further decoration

small doll or figure for Goldilocks
3 small flat wood scraps for the beds—small, medium, and large
3 wood scrap cubes for the chairs—small, medium, and large
1 larger wood scrap for the table
3 bowls made from buttons
glue
permanent markers for decorating wood
piece of felt for main cottage area
felt scraps for carpeting and blankets
fabric scraps for decorating beds, table

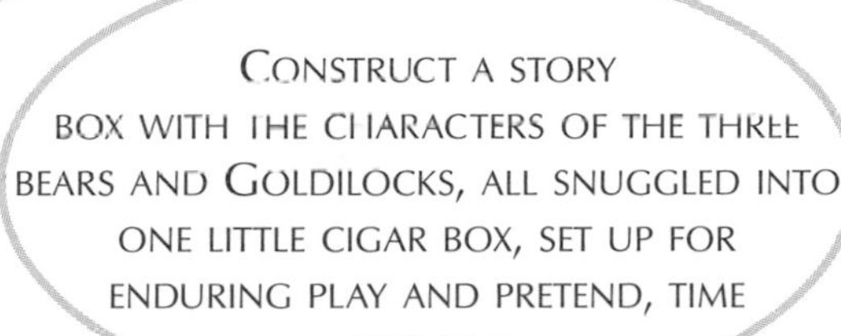

Steps

- Read *Goldilocks and the Three Bears* by Jan Brett or any other author. There are many different books with beautiful, imaginative illustrations from which to choose.
- Collect all the materials for making the story box. The box will be for storage, but can also be a playhouse or stage for the toys to act out the story.
- Goldilocks will be a small doll or figurine. If none are available, construct a Goldilocks from an empty spool of thread adorned with yarn or felt hair and clothing. Draw facial features with markers. For the bears, find three bear toys, or construct them out of empty spools adorned again with felt scraps.

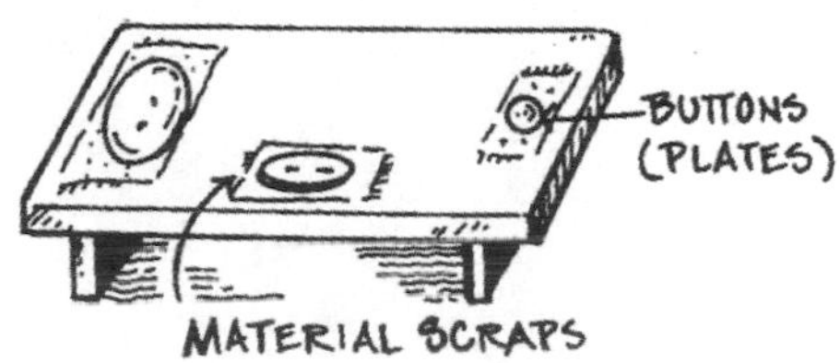

- Select a piece of fabric or felt that will be the "cottage floor" of the three bears' home. It should be large enough to spread out the beds, chairs, and table with bowls. Set aside.
- Decorate the three beds (three flat rectangle scraps of wood, from small to larger) by gluing on felt or fabric. Use permanent markers to add details. Make little pillows and blankets from fabric too.
- Use a block of wood as a table. Glue on three little fabric scrap placemats, if desired. Make the chairs from wood scrap cubes, in three sizes. Decorate with fabric scraps, or draw decorations with markers. Find three buttons to set the table with the bears' bowls of porridge.
- Spread out the felt cottage floor. Arrange the three bears' house. Play "Goldilocks and the Three Bears," reciting the story aloud, or playing with the figures in imaginative ways.

More Ideas

Make story boxes for any favorite tales, poems, songs, or stories. Keep handy for independent play and pretend.

Enjoy playing the Three Bears and Goldilocks characters with puppets, flannel board, or costumes.

Let's Play Make-Believe

Chapter 6

The ABC's of Make-Believe
Let's Play Artist
Let's Play School
Let's Play Birthday
Let's Play Tea Party
Let's Play Office
Let's Play Window Washer
Let's Play Baby Nursery
Let's Play Carpenter
Let's Play Theater
Let's Play Bank
Let's Play Fix-It Shop
Let's Play Scientist
Let's Play Beach
Let's Play Buried Treasure
Let's Play Camp Out
Let's Play Florist
Let's Play Veterinarian
Let's Play Astronaut
Let's Play Fast Food Restaurant

The ABC's of Make-Believe

Pretend and make-believe is everything from playing house or playing with dolls and trucks to planning a tea party on the lawn. Dramatic play is good for social, psychological, and cognitive development. Here is a list of imaginative themes from A to Z. Start with something especially easy (these are marked with * and many are included in this chapter). When you are comfortable with setting up simple dramatic play areas, move on to something more challenging.

A

airplane and airport
animal shelter
*animals: pretend to be—pets, jungle, wild, farm, forest
aquarium
art gallery
*artist
astronaut

B

*baby nursery
baby's bath
bakery
*bank
barnyard
beach
beauty shop
* bedroom
birthday party
book store
bowling
buried treasure/pirate
* bus

C

camping
candy shop
car wash
card shop
*carpenter/wood worker/furniture maker
castle
cave
circus
computer store
construction
covered wagon
cowboys
countries: Japan, Mexico, China, more

D

daddy shaving
dancer
dentist office (on dolls, not real kids)
department store
dish washing
* doctor
dress-up
drive-in restaurant

E

Easter bunny egg painting studio
electronics company (computers, keyboards, toggle switches, disks)
exercise club

F

factory/assembly line
fairy tale land
* family
farm
fast-food restaurant
film maker
fire station
fish market
* fishing
* fix-it shop
florist/flower store

G

garage/car repair
gardening
gas station
gift shop
gift wrapping
grocery store

H

hairdresser
Halloween/costume shop
hardware store
holidays
hospital
hot air balloon
* house/housekeeping/ family
hundred acre woods

I

ice cream truck
ice cream shop/fountain
igloo

J

janitor
jets
jewelry making
junk shop

K

karate/martial arts
kindergarten

L

landscaper/yard work
laundry
* library
log cabin
long house

M

magic
magic carpet
make-up/face painting
martial arts/karate
mermaid grotto
motorcycle shop
movie theater
museum

N

newspaper office
night and day
north pole
nursery
nursery rhymes play

O

ocean
* office
outer space

P

paleontologist
parade
park
pet shop
photographer
picnic
pirate ship
pirates/buried treasure
pizza parlor
planetarium/observatory

playdough cooking, baking
plumber
police station
post office
puppet show/puppet theater

Q

quilt shop

R

radio station
* rain
rain forest/jungle
ranch
ranger station
recycling depot
restaurant
rock museum
rocket
royalty/kings and queens

S

sailing/boats
sandwich shop
Santa's workshop
* school
school bus
* scientist
shoe repair
* shoeshine
shoe store
sidewalk art sale
space station
* storybooks: classics (Little Red Riding Hood, Three Little Pigs, others)
storyteller

T

* tea party
teacher
television station
* theater
toy store
train
treasure island
TV newscast
TV weather forecast

U

under the sea

V

vacation/travel
veterinarian office
voting

W

wash day
weather station/weather forecast
wedding
western day
winter wonderland

X, Y, Z

zoo

Let's Play Artist

10

Start with the basics, then change the art supplies to change the artistic make-believe from painter to potter to sculptor.

The Basics

drawing and painting paper
paint and brushes
crayons, markers, pencils
scissors
glue, paste, tape, stapler, hole punch, pushpins
playdough
smock, paint shirt, or apron

Steps

- For beginners, start with the materials listed above, then add or change one or two materials to keep play interesting as days or weeks go by. Many suggestions are listed below. There are many long term possibilities.
- Set up and arrange an art area centered around a work table. Store supplies in containers on the table, on the floor, or on a nearby shelf. The idea is to use materials that are on hand rather than buying anything new.
- Artists like to pretend to be great masters and wear a beret, smock, and hold a palette in one hand. (Always hold the palette in the nonpainting hand.) Hang posters or prints of great artwork around the area.
- Finished artwork can go to a display area for viewing or sales. Have a gallery showing!

More Ideas

Because artists like to do more than paint, here are some basic art ideas to choose from

still-life sketch–draw a vase of flowers with pencils on big white paper
crayon resist–color with crayons and paint over the drawing with thin black watercolors or tempera
portrait–look at someone's face, and paint, draw, or color their image in any style
wood scrap sculpture–glue wood scraps together, and paint when glue is set
sewing poster–sew with yarn in a big needle through holes punched around the edge of a cardboard shape
collage–glue anything on anything

combine any of the above, like a wood scrap sculpture that is a portrait with collage materials

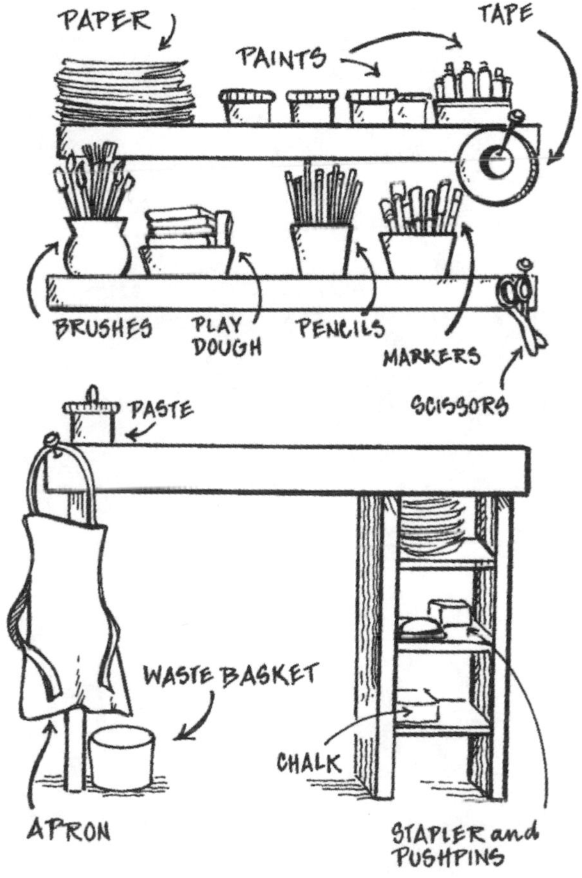

Additional Materials

paint easel with paint cups

NOTE: OR FOLD A PIECE OF CARDBOARD IN A TENT SHAPE AND TAPE IT TO A WORK TABLE. TAPE SUBSTITUTE EASEL TO THE CARDBOARD TENT.

beret

paint palette (make one from cardboard)

posters, prints, postcards of great art works

choice of paper

art tissue • butcher paper • cardboard scraps • clear contact paper • construction paper fabric as paper • foil paper • large newsprint sheet • magazine pictures • matte board scraps • old posters • scraps from frame shop • scraps from printer's shop

display areas for finished art, such as

clothespins on a wire or rope • empty frames for paintings • fish net on wall with clothespins • magnets on a refrigerator • shelf for sculptures • strip of wood on wall with pushpins

art supplies, such as

clay tools • colored chalk • colored pencils • needle and thread • palette knife or spatula for mixing paint • self-hardening clay or baking clay • watercolor paints and brushes

collage materials for gluing, stored in containers and boxes, such as

beads, jewelry • bottle caps • buttons • cotton balls • feathers • glitter labels • leather scraps • leaves • pine cones • seeds • sewing trims • shredded paper stickers • tiles • weeds • wood shavings • yarn

Let's Play School

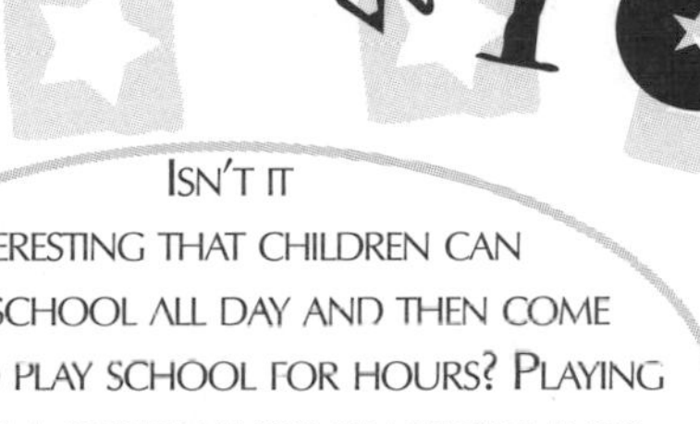

Isn't it interesting that children can go to school all day and then come home and play school for hours? Playing school is a great way to practice things already learned, learn new things, or teach things to others.

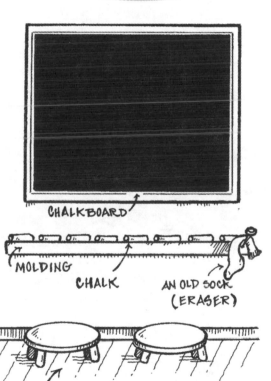

The Basics

chalkboard and chalk, dry-erase board and markers, or square of cardboard and chalk
paper
crayons, pens, pencils, erasers
chalk, chalk board, eraser
desks, tables, chairs, or boxes
favorite dolls or toys as students

Steps

- Set up a school area with a chalkboard, dry erase board, or square of cardboard as the center of learning. (Chalk will wipe off of the cardboard nicely. Dry erase boards work well with markers. Use an old sock for the eraser.) Place boxes or chairs around the board, or set up desks or boxes for desks.
- Everyone sits at a table or desk, and children take turns being the teacher.
- If stuffed toys are attending school, encourage them to try hard and they will get a sticker for work well done!

More Ideas

Play school in all its wide variety of activities, like

art • gym time • lunch or snack • math • nap time • recess
singing, dancing • walk to school or ride in a play bus or car • writing and reading

Additional Materials

bell to ring
books to read
clock
colored stick-on stars
flag for pledge of allegiance
learning games
music/tapes for singing time
new or used books, like
mazes • follow the dots • paperdolls
stickers

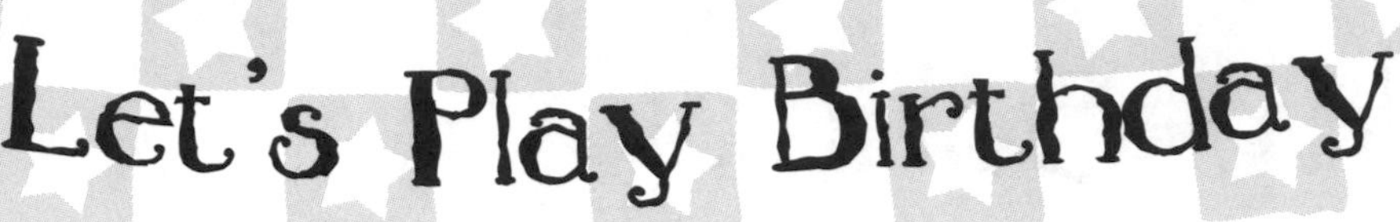

Let's Play Birthday

PLAY SIMPLE BIRTHDAY PRETEND, WITH A PLAY CAKE AND PRESENTS; OR PLAY ELABORATE BIRTHDAY PRETEND, WITH CARD MAKING, GIFT-WRAPPING, CAKE DECORATING, AND MORE.

The Basics

table and chairs
playdough
birthday candles
art materials as needed, such as
crayons, glue, markers, paper, scissors, and tape
crepe paper and balloons, optional

Steps

- Celebrate the birthday (or unbirthday) of a friend, family member, pet, or favorite toy. Make invitations with paper and markers, if desired.
- Set up a table and chairs.
- Decorate the room with crepe paper and balloons, if desired.
- Make a cake out of playdough with real candles stuck into it. Decorate the cake with any collage items to make it pretty. (Do not eat, of course.)
- Enjoy the pretend cake, and sing "Happy Birthday."

More Ideas

Wrap boxes so the lids come off, so they can be opened again and again. It's fun to put in small toys or other pretend gifts.
Create birthday cards on heavy card stock paper. Old birthday cards can also be cut and pasted to create new designs.
Play party games like "Pin the Tail on the Donkey."
Make a real cake to eat, and other authentic party experiences. Consider having adult-supervised candles to blow out.

Additional Materials

dress-up clothes for parties
games to play
gift bags or fancy boxes
party favors and prizes
party plates, napkins, cups, plastic silverware, tablecloth
ribbons and bows
used birthday cards, or hand made

Let's Play Tea Party

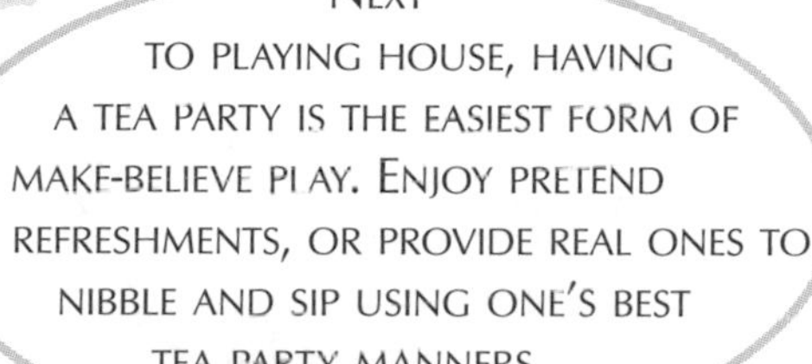

Next
to playing house, having
a tea party is the easiest form of
make-believe play. Enjoy pretend
refreshments, or provide real ones to
nibble and sip using one's best
tea party manners.

The Basics

tea set (child size or full adult size), including cups, saucers, spoons, teapot, sugar bowl, creamer pitcher
table and chairs (use stools, boxes, blocks, or other furniture props)
real or pretend tea, water, juice, or other liquid
real or pretend cake, cookies, crackers, or small sandwiches
stuffed animals or dolls as additional guests
good manners

Steps

- Prepare a small table for a tea party. Have enough chairs for each person or toy invited. Cover the table with a tablecloth, or set out place mats. (Sheets of paper work nicely for mats.)
- Set out the tea set, napkins, plates, and whatever other selection of items there might be. Make it look pretty.
- One person will be the host, and the others will be guests. The host is in charge of pouring tea and serving food to the guests, though they may take turns.
- Engage in polite conversation about how good the tea tastes, how lovely the flowers are, what a nice day it is, and so forth.
- Good guests often help clean up when the party is over. Set up a dish washing area, if desired.

More Ideas

Play Royal Tea with a king or queen in charge of the royal guests, all very so so and lah-tee-dah!
Spend some time making cookies, cakes, or sandwiches in fancy little shapes for a real tea party.
Have a Teddy Bear Tea or a real tea for Mother's Day.

Additional Materials

dish washing area, with cleaning supplies like sponges, towels, waste basket
napkins, cloth or paper, place mats, small plates, tablecloth
real or pretend sugar cubes
vase with real or pretend flowers (or weeds), or paper or plastic flowers

1

Let's Play Office

THE PROPS FOR PLAYING OFFICE, WHETHER MANY OR ONLY A FEW, ARE EASY TO FIND AND HIGHLY MOTIVATIONAL FOR DETAILED DRAMATIC PLAY.

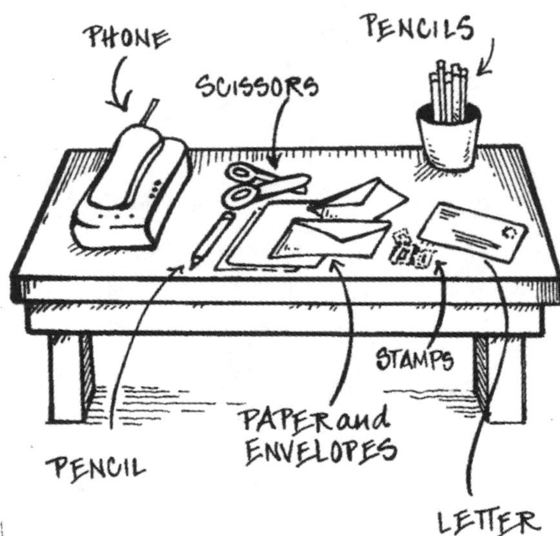

The Basics

pens, pencils
tape, stapler
paper, envelopes stickers for stamps
telephones (two is better than one)
desk and chairs (or boxes)

Steps

- Set up a desk or table as the central prop, and organize the rest of the office around it.
- Arrange envelopes, stamps, and paper for letter writing.
- Prepare the desk with a few office props.
- If desired, have refreshments like coffee and tea on hand.
- Spend time working very hard in the office.
- When the day is over, it's time to go home from work.

More Ideas

Put up a sign to tell what kind of office this is: insurance, real estate, accounting, school, and so on. Find specific props to make this office function according to its type.

Incorporate playing "Family" or "House" where family members go off to work at the office.

Additional Materials

office and desk supplies, such as
  big envelopes • boxes • clip board • scissors, hole punch
  boxes to make into (draw knobs and buttons on them to resemble the machines)
  computer • copy machine • cubby holes/mail slots • file drawers • scanner • trash can
clock (old clock for play, or make one from cardboard with movable hands)
old typewriter
coffee cups, pot, accessories
adding machine or calculator
photograph of family member for desk

Let's Play Window Washer

1

WASHING WINDOWS, INSIDE AND OUT, INVOLVES ELBOW GREASE AND REMARKABLE PROPS WITH NAMES AND WORDS LIKE SQUEEGEE, PUMP, SQUIRT, AND POLISH.

The Basics

soft cloths or rags, made from
baby diapers • old pajamas • old towels • T-shirts • underwear
sponge
window cleaner (real or pretend)
squeegee
small bucket
water

Steps

- Begin washing windows at child height. First spray and sponge, then squeegee windows clean. Wipe dry.
- Outdoor windows may also need work.
- Mirrors, table tops, and even floors may need cleaning.
- If desired, write up pretend bills for the window washing service, and have the customer pay by check, cash, or credit card.
- When the job is done, walk about and inspect the work. There might be some that needs redoing!

More Ideas

Go outdoors with a bucket of water, sponges, towels, and squeegees, and clean doorsteps, signs, curbs, and anything that needs washing.

Additional Materials

apron
pad of paper and pencil
play money and coins, old checkbook, or pretend credit card for payment
pump spray window cleaner
small ladder or step-stool (supervise closely)

1 Let's Play Baby Nursery

EVERYONE WAS A BABY AT ONE TIME (NOT LONG AGO FOR SOME!), SO PLAY IS FROM RECENT MEMORY AND OFTEN QUITE REALISTIC.

The Basics

baby dolls
baby bottles
baby blankets
doll crib or cradle toy, or make one from boxes
doll clothes
small tub, water, baby shampoo, optional
pictures of babies

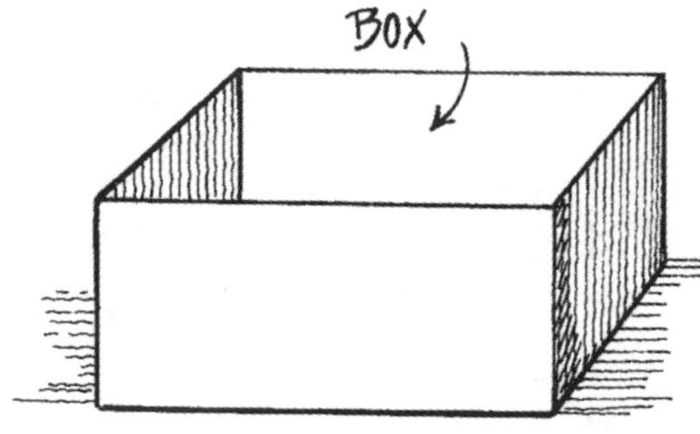

Steps

- Set up a corner as a baby nursery, for newborns only, or for babies of all ages and needs. (Make cradles from cardboard boxes lined with blankets for sleepy babies.)
- Some of the baby activities possible might include
  Burp • Change diapers • Feed with bottles • Feed with spoons from dishes that are filled from empty baby food jars • Play patty-cake, so-big, peekaboo and other baby games
  Read to baby • Rock to sleep • Sing to sleep • Soothe away tears • Tuck in bed
- For extra fun, fill a water table or small tub with water. Wash and dry the babies using baby shampoo and fluffy baby towels. Mmm, babies smell so sweet!

NOTE: DOLLS MUST BE WASHABLE FOR THE BATH ACTIVITY.

- Look at pictures of babies and what they do for more ideas.

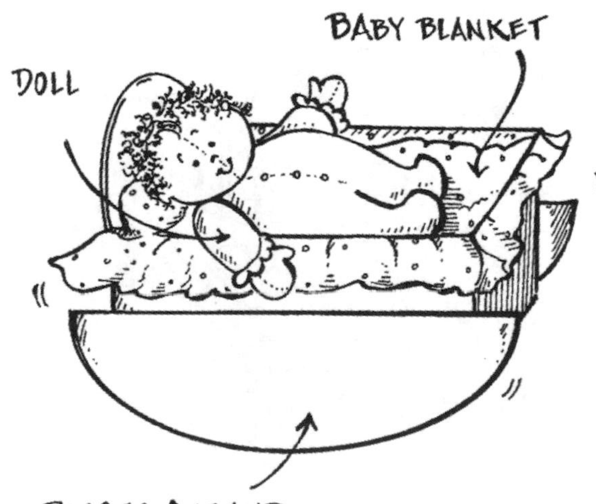

More Ideas

Hold a real baby with the parent's permission and assistance.
Look at baby pictures of when you were little.
Sing to a real baby, play peekaboo, or play patty cake.

Additional Materials

baby books
baby wipes
bibs
car seats
diapers (and extra tape)
empty baby food jars
pacifier for dolls
rattles, toy key ring, other baby toys
real rocking chair
songs to sing
spoons and dishes
empty lotion, powder, and baby wash bottles

Let's Play Carpenter

Working with wood is filled with pounding and sanding, and very important tools!

The Basics

sturdy work table
wood scraps, all shapes and sizes
sandpaper
hammers, saws
nails, many different types (short ones with large heads work very well)
goggles
wood glue

Steps

- Find a sturdy work table at child height that is able to take some hammering and nailing, sanding and painting.
- Arrange the supplies in boxes or on a shelf near the work table. Stack wood scraps underneath the table in boxes.
- Begin woodworking. Some of the activities that might occur are
  drilling holes for screws • hammering and nailing • measuring • painting • sanding
  screwing in wood screws
- Make real things, or simply work with wood.

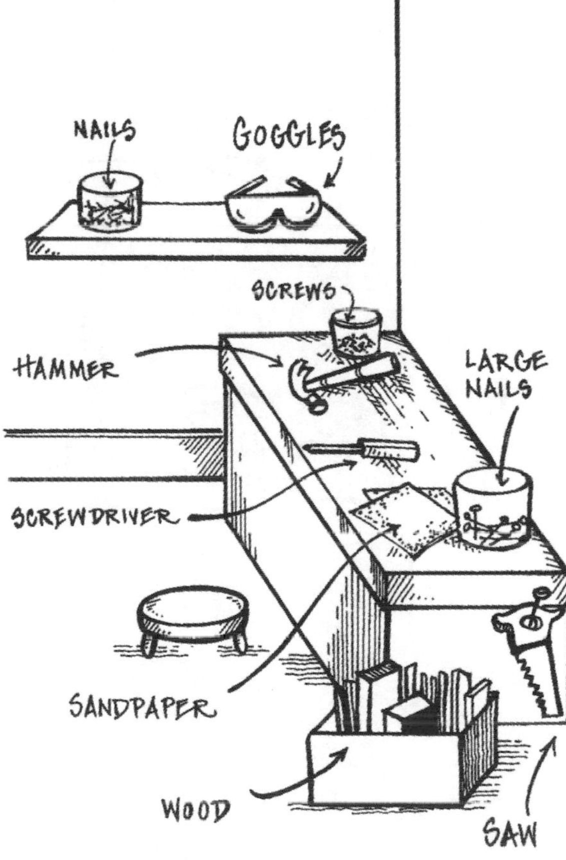

More Ideas

Set up a furniture-making shop that sells furniture for dolls or favorite toys.
Make actual things out of wood like
bird house • book ends • napkin holder

Additional Materials

carpenter's apron or tool belt
carpenter's pencil
colored masking tape
filter masks
gold paint and brush, optional
ruler
screwdrivers and other tools
tape measure
tool box
wood putty
wood screws
working hand drill

2 Let's Play Theater

START WITH THE BASIC EXPERIENCE OF "GOING TO THE MOVIES," THEN EXPAND PLAY TO REAL SHOWS, PLAYS, RECITATIONS, OR CONCERTS STAGED BY YOUNG PERFORMING ARTISTS.

The Basics

choice of theater for set-up
movie theater: white sheet or paper on wall, or VCR and movie on tape
puppet theater: puppets, puppet stage (see Chapter 3 for ideas)
plays, concerts, recitations, or other shows: stage area, costumes, or props
chairs: chairs, carpet squares, boxes, blocks
tickets: real ones, or play tickets cut from heavy paper

Steps

Going to the pretend Movies will be used for a beginner theater suggestion:

- Pin a white sheet or big rectangle of white paper to the wall for a pretend movie screen. Arrange chairs or carpet scraps to simulate a theater.
- Decide beforehand what the pretend movie is, and pretend it is funny, scary, sad, and so on.

HINT: MOVIE-GOERS ESPECIALLY SEEM TO ENJOY WATCHING SCARY MOVIES!

- Put up a poster announcing the movie showing tonight.
- Make paper scrap tickets for the movie-goers to purchase.
- Turn the lights down low and let the show begin. Natural pretending will take its course.
- When the show is over, turn the lights up and head on home!

More Ideas

Suggestions for different types of theater ideas
Put on a puppet show (see Chapter 3 for puppetry ideas).
Recite a nursery rhyme. Wear simple dress-up clothes or carry a simple prop. For example, Jack Be Nimble would need a candlestick to jump over.
Act out a simple fairy tale, nursery rhyme, or poem.
Dress up like a favorite book character and tell the story.
Perform favorite songs or make up a dance to perform.
Perform a flannel board story show.
Put on a more elaborate play, with costumes, programs, and invited guests. Plays can be original or from favorite books or movies.

Additional Materials

art supplies to make tickets, programs, signs, such as
  crayons • glue • markers • paper • scissors • stapler • tape
lighting, optional
  flashlight • desk lamp • Christmas tree lights
play cash register and play money
poster
  announcing show or movie
pretend snacks
  paper sacks (popcorn) • paper cups (pop)
programs
  pretend programs of plain folded paper or designed with actual show information, or programs saved from real shows
sign
  banner • cardboard sign • playbills to post
ticket booth
  cardboard box • small table • or shelf

★ 2 Let's Play Bank

GATHER THE PROPS FOR THIS MAKE-BELIEVE ACTIVITY AND SET THEM UP AROUND A TELLER'S TABLE. EVERYONE CAN BE QUITE BUSINESS-LIKE AND GROWN UP, ESPECIALLY IF THERE ARE DRESS-UP CLOTHES TO WEAR.

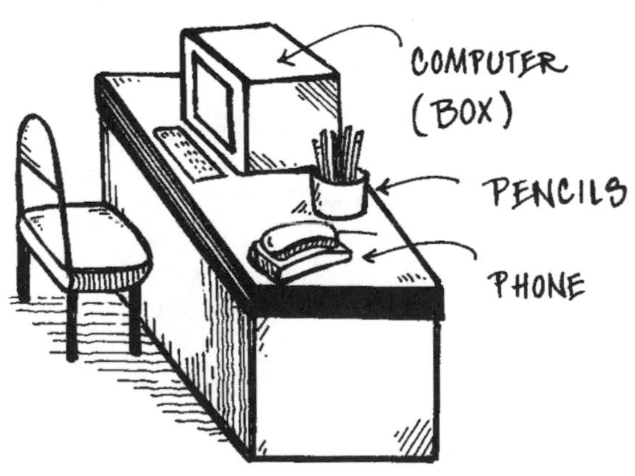

The Basics

table and chairs or boxes

large quantity of play money (Photocopy real money and cut out, use play money from games like Monopoly, or draw money on slips of paper. Poker chips, bingo markers, and buttons make good coins.)

cardboard computer

pencils, pens, scrap paper

telephones

art supplies like crayons, markers, glue, tape, and scissors

Steps

- Set up a play corner centered around the teller's table and a desk and chair.
- Some of the bank people would be teller, bank president, loan representative, and customer. Take turns playing different parts.
- Bank play will depend on experience. It may be as simple as depositing money or writing a check. Some of the on-going business at a bank includes

  deposit money • withdraw money • write checks • put valuables in a safety deposit box • take out a loan for a car • finance a home
- Take turns with different bank jobs.

More Ideas

Play Bank and Store at the same time, writing checks or withdrawing money from the bank to go to the store and buy things.

Save money towards buying something special. Keep track of how much money is being saved.

Count a can full of pennies, stacking the pennies in piles of ten.

Additional Materials

adding machines • calculators • cash box with money tray • checkbooks • desk and chair
gold bricks (painted blocks of wood) • money bags • pencil tied to yarn and taped to table
play credit cards and card machine • safe (cardboard box with lock drawn on it)
safety deposit boxes (shoeboxes with numbers written on them) • savings books

Let's Play Fix-it-Shop

Everyone loves the repair shop—a place to fix things or just take them apart! Include tins full of nuts, bolts, screws, and washers to work with.

The Basics

sturdy work table
choices of tools, various sizes and types
    duct tape • hammer • masking tape
    measuring tape • pliers • ruler
    scissors • screwdriver • wrenches
muffin tin filled with choices of
    bolts • nails of all kinds • nuts
other hardware bits and pieces
    screws of all kinds • washers of all sizes
work gloves
used or broken things to repair (all electric cords removed) such as
    adding machine • clock • coffee maker
    computer • hairdryer • iron
    locks • mixer • radio • tape recorder
    telephone • toaster • toys • vacuum

Steps

- Set up a sturdy work table that can be hammered and bumped. Arrange the work materials under the table, on a shelf, or in boxes on the floor. A muffin tin filled with hardware can sit right on the table.
- Begin working on things like a toaster or a telephone. Taking them apart is most of the fun. Sometimes things can go back together again too!
- Customers in the fix-it shop can pretend to pick up fixed items and pay with play money for work done. Fix-it-shop workers can write up orders and ring up sales on a play cash register.
- Fix-it shops can also sell fixed items.

More Ideas

Set up a car repair shop with car parts, tools, mechanic's suits to cover clothing, and so on. Include a nail brush and some of that rough soap that takes off grease.
A toy shop is similar to a fix-it shop or a carpenter's shop. Build, sell, and repair toys.

Additional Materials

blocks of packing Styrofoam, for hammering, nailing, cutting
cash register made from a box, play money, pad of paper and pencil for writing up orders
clean tins for storage of hardware and scraps, from coffee, tuna, soup, juice
glue, tape, markers, stapler, scissors, hole punch

Let's Play Scientist

SCIENTIFIC PROPS CAN BE EXTREMELY IMAGINARY, LIKE USING AN OLD PHONE CORD TO SIMULATE A TUBE OF PRETEND MYSTERIOUS LIQUID OR A JAR OF COLORED WATER TO FABRICATE A SECRET FORMULA.

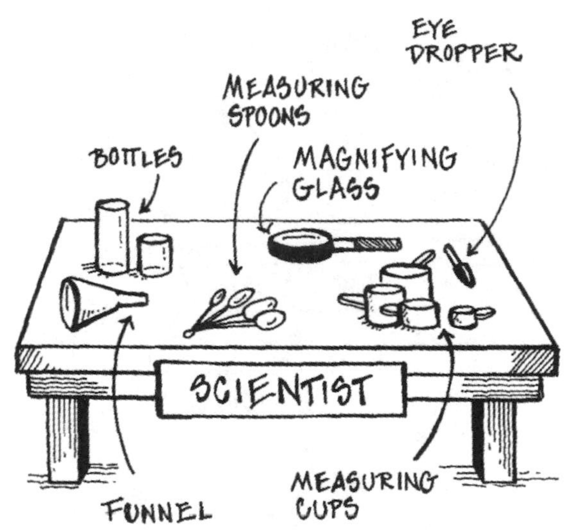

The Basics

table or workspace
choice of utensils for research (one or two to start)
  bottles • funnels • jars, cups, containers • kitchen utensils and tools • measuring cups
  measuring spoons • plastic containers • spray bottle • stir sticks • thermometer
water (plain and colored)
rubber tubing
telephone
eyedropper
magnifying glass
paper towels
materials to help study and research (one or two to start)
  clipboard • clock • lab coat • pens, pencils, paper • ruler, protractor • timer

Steps

- Set up and assemble choices of materials on the table or work space.
- Explore, study, and experiment with the materials.
- Calculate experiments.
- Keep records of discoveries on paper.
- Mix and measure.
- Share findings and discoveries.

NOTE: SCIENTISTS ALSO LIKE TO CONCOCT IMAGINATIVE EXPERIMENTS WITH THINGS LIKE FLOUR, COLORED WATER, GLITTER, OR OTHER CHOICES OF MIXABLE MATERIALS.

Additional Materials

scientific equipment, such as
  calculator • computer (made from a box) • egg timer • microscope (made from toilet paper tube) • PCV pipe scraps • plastic slides • rubber bands • spiral telephone cord
  string • telephone(s) • telescope (made from toilet paper tubes) • wood blocks • lamp
materials to motivate study, research, and experimenting, such as
  geographical map • leaves, pressed flowers • models of bones, heart, ear, eye, etc.
  pictures of things to study • pictures to put under microscope • shells • star map

Let's Play Beach

2

THE BEACH OR THE SEASHORE—EVEN THE LAKE, RIVER, POND, OR CREEK—ALL EVOKE PLAYING, PICNICKING, AND FROLICKING. IT MAKES US THINK OF SUNSHINE, WATER, AND FUN.

The Basics

shells or stones
clean sand contained
in a sandbox • on a tarp • in a large, shallow cardboard box
or use a yellow or white blanket or sheet as the play sand
set up the beach outdoors instead with sand poured directly on the ground or in a sandbox
sand toys, bucket shovel

Steps

- Prepare a make-believe beach. Spread out a tarp with the edges pulled up and fill with clean sand, or fill an indoor sandbox. A less messy and still highly imaginative idea is to spread out a white or yellow blanket or sheet as make-believe sand.
- Set up assorted props to make the beach scene complete, such as buckets, shovels, towel, hat, and sunglasses, as listed in the materials.
- Now, enjoy the beach!

  Pretend to swim in the ocean.
  Are there any imaginary sea creatures in sight?
  Run from the waves.
  Search for shells and treasures.
  Have a play or real picnic on the towel.
  Read a book near the shore.
  Walk on the beach.
  Make a shell collection.
  Pretend to be lost at the seashore and camp out until help arrives.

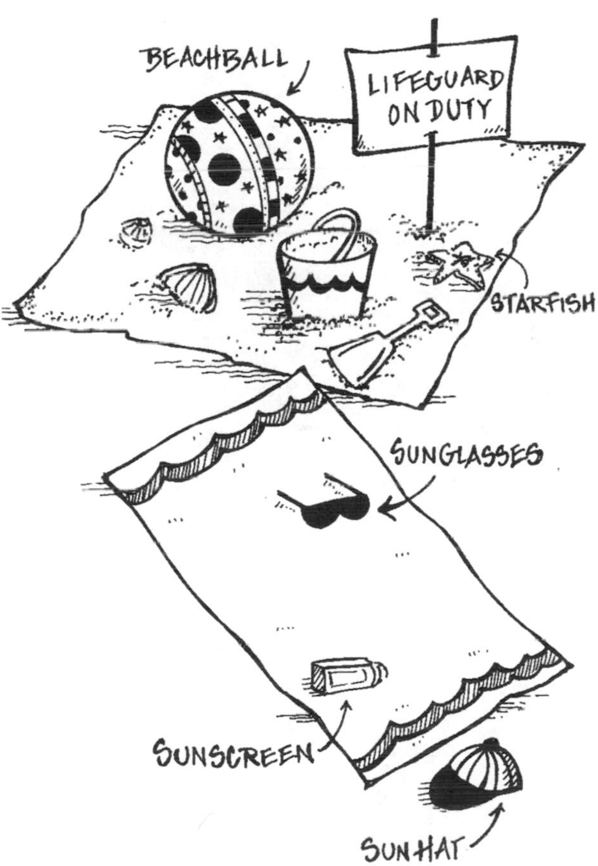

Additional Materials

bathing suit or sun outfit, optional • beach ball • beach chair • beach shoes or sandals
beach towel • binoculars (make from paper towel tubes) • books, magazines, playing cards
coral • driftwood • favorite toys or dolls • fishing gear • inflatable boat or plastic boat
life preservers • picnic basket or cooler chest, with pretend or real food, empty soda bottles
plastic sea-life toys like starfish, fish, crabs, worms • pretend sunscreen or lotion
sand dollars • signs like "No Dogs Allowed" or "Lifeguard on Duty"
sun hat • sunglasses • swimming gear • umbrella

2 Let's Play Buried Treasure

Follow the treasure map to the buried treasure! Hooray, we're rich! Bury the treasure in a new hiding place, and start all over again.

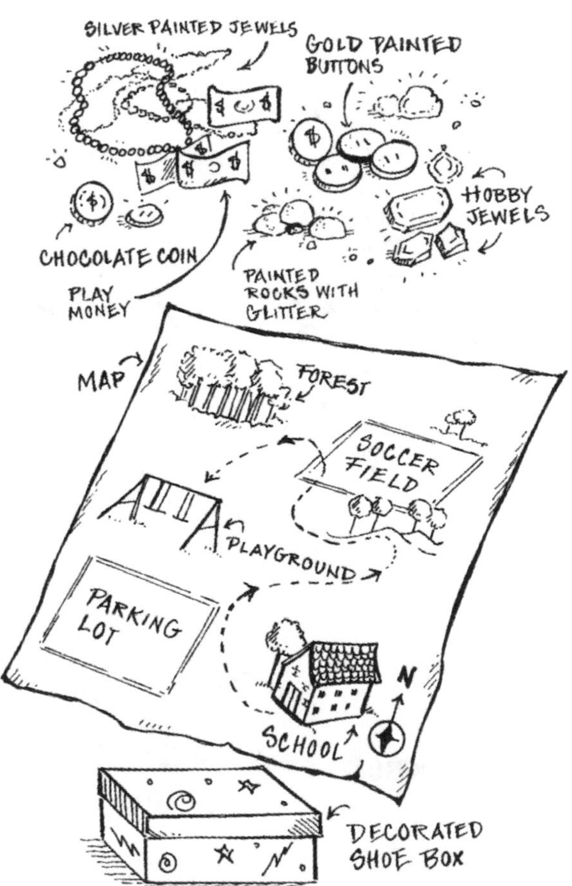

The Basics

collect and assemble items as the pretend treasure (one or two to start)
beads and hobby jewels • chocolate coins wrapped in foil • large buttons
old jewelry • plastic beads on strings • play money • small figurines or statues
small rocks • small wood scraps
gold, silver, other metallic spray or brush-on paints
glitter, glitter paint, glitter glue, sequins
box for treasure chest
newspaper to protect table during painting
paint and brushes
paper and pens for drawing map
used wet tea bag

Steps

- Prepare the treasures. Some suggestions are
  - Paint the rocks gold and silver.
  - Paint the small statues gold.
  - Cover the wood scraps with glitter.
  - Cover large buttons with glitter paint.
- Dry the painted items. Spread out the other items and decide what will be in the treasure chest that will be buried.
- Select a wooden or cardboard box for the treasure chest. The treasures can be hidden or buried in the chest, or the chest can be used to collect them after each one is found. Decorate the chest with markers and paint in any design.
- Find a place to bury the treasures like a sandbox, soft dirt in a garden, or behind a couch.
- Draw a treasure map that leads the seekers to the buried treasure. Wipe the map with a wet, used tea bag to make it look like old parchment.
- Find the treasure! Bury the treasure again in a new place, and start all over again.

More Ideas

Pretend to be pirates. Dress like pirates (eye patch, skull cap, rolled-up pants, scars, earrings), talk like pirates (Avast me hearties! Ahoy there! Surrender ye swabs! Scupper that ship! Land ho!) and sing like pirates (Yo ho, yo ho, the pirate's life for me....).

Design flags, make sea biscuits, write with invisible ink.

Let's Play Camp Out

2 ★★

GOING CAMPING INDOORS IS SIMILAR TO PLAYING HOUSE, BUT WITH MORE CAPTIVATING PLAY IDEAS AND EXCITEMENT, ESPECIALLY IF THE LIGHTS ARE TURNED OUT WHEN IT IS PRETEND NIGHTTIME!

The Basics

tent ideas, such as
- blanket or sheet over a table, reaching to the floor • real tent • rope tied between two objects, sheet draped over the rope • teepee

sleeping equipment, such as
- blanket • pillow • sleeping bag • tarp • flashlight • books, playing cards

Steps

- Set up a tent in a corner of the room, or, if no tent materials are available, camp out in the wide open without a tent!
- Set up the sleeping area in the tent, or on the ground near the fire.
- Play camp out! Some of the activities that might occur are
  - being afraid of forest animals • pretend thunderstorms • reading in the tent by flashlight real naps • setting up camp over and over • sleeping • telling scary stories
- When camping is over, pack up and head back home.

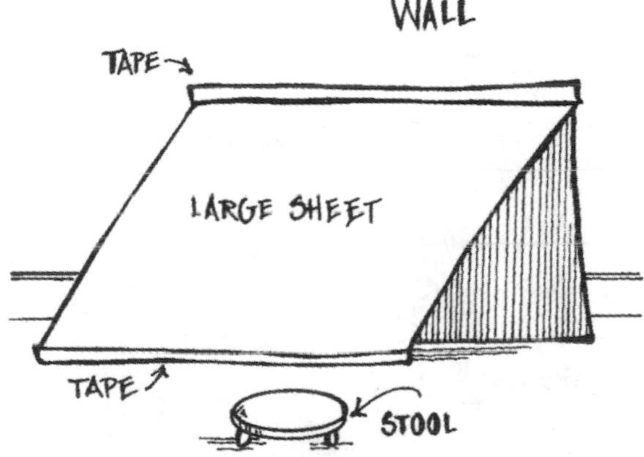

More Ideas

Really camp out, too!

Sing cowboy songs; pretend to be cowboys, play rodeo, or have western related play.

Have a square dance.

Stuff red and orange tissue into the play campfire for pretend hot coals.

Build up the campfire with rocks or blocks. Place a cooling rack across the pretend fire for coffee pot or frying pan.

Additional Materials

blocks or stools to sit on
books, playing cards
camping equipment, such as
- backpack • canteen or thermos

cooking equipment (pan, spoon, pot)
picnic things (cooler chest, basket)
marshmallows for play toasting, optional
pretend campfire props, such as
- logs • paper flames taped on
- rocks to line fire • toothpicks for matches

favorite toys (as forest animals or as friends)

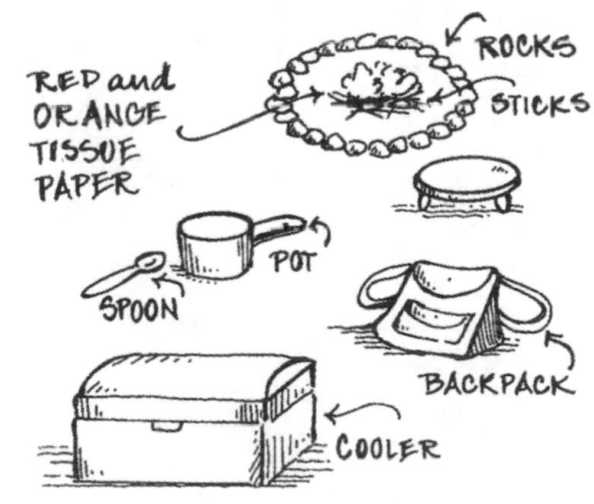

2

Let's Play Florist

PLAYING FLORIST OFFERS CREATIVE AS WELL AS VALUABLE BUSINESS PLAY. USING REAL FLOWERS MAKES THIS PRETEND ACTIVITY CLOSER TO THE REAL THING, BUT PLASTIC ONES LAST LONGER AND CAN BE USED OVER AND OVER AGAIN.

The Basics

work table
soil in water table or plastic trays
pots, cups, vases, baskets, milk cartons
and containers of all kinds
live or plastic flowers and plants
ribbons and raffia
small cards or old greeting cards with flowers
stickers for prices
art supplies as needed, such as
crayons • markers • scissors • glue • tape
stapler • paper
telephone

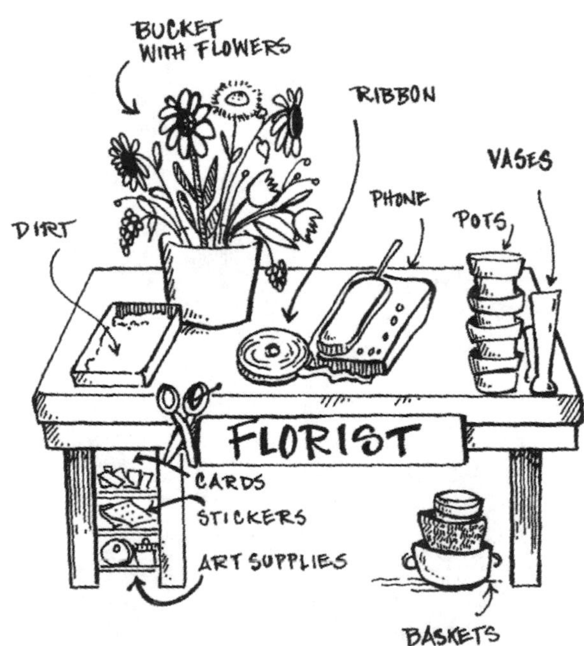

Steps

- Set up a work table for arranging flowers as well as planting and caring for them.
- Take orders on the phone, arrange special orders, or make arrangements that will be for sale in the florist shop.
- Arrange flowers in pots with soil, or in vases with water. If possible, acquire some live flowers or plants for display or arranging too. Tie ribbons or raffia on the arrangements. Display them for sale. Decorate greeting cards for sale. Make price stickers.
- Sell flowers and flower arrangements to customers. Flower arrangements make nice decorations for dining tables, windowsills, or for parties.
- Take arrangements apart and play florist all over again.

More Ideas

Make flowers out of
cupcake cups glued on sticks • dyed coffee filters on pipe cleaners • paper for blossoms and wire for stems.
Make dried flowers or pressed flowers.

Additional Materials

books about flowers • brochures from florists • cash register made from cardboard box
gardening gloves • note pad and pencil for orders • pictures of flowers • play money
shallow cardboard boxes for transporting pots or displaying plants • smocks or aprons
tissue or newsprint to wrap flowers • watering can

Let's Play Veterinarian

2 ★★

Playing veterinarian is a highly imaginative pretend time where children can work miracles on stuffed animals while exploring thoughts and fears about visiting the pediatrician.

The Basics

stuffed toy dogs and cats, bunnies, etc.
medical tools or supplies (real or hand made), such as
ace bandage • Band-Aids • cotton balls • empty lotion bottle • empty pill bottle
stethoscope • surgical gown and cap • tape (masking tape) • thermometer
tongue depressors • toy doctor kit supplies • table • telephone

Steps

- Playing vet is very much like playing doctor, except the focus is on a pet, not a person. This is precisely why children love to explore the medical aspects of examining and treating a toy pet—they are often basing their experiences on themselves and their own visits to the pediatrician.
- Set up a vet's office centered around the examining table.
- Have toy pets visit the vet for examining and treatment. Some of the situations that often evolve in play are
  broken bones • cuts or bruises • diseases • hurt head, ear, eye, leg, foot, paw, tummy
  loneliness • needs a family (lives at the pound, is lost, is abandoned)
- Often prescriptions or appointments are needed, including telephone calls and detailed consultations and treatments. Return visits are common.

Additional materials

animal X-rays (donated by local vet office)
cardboard boxes for animal carry cases, kennels
clipboard
doggie biscuits or other pet treats
notebook and pencil
pretend X-ray machine (made from cardboard box)
weighing scale

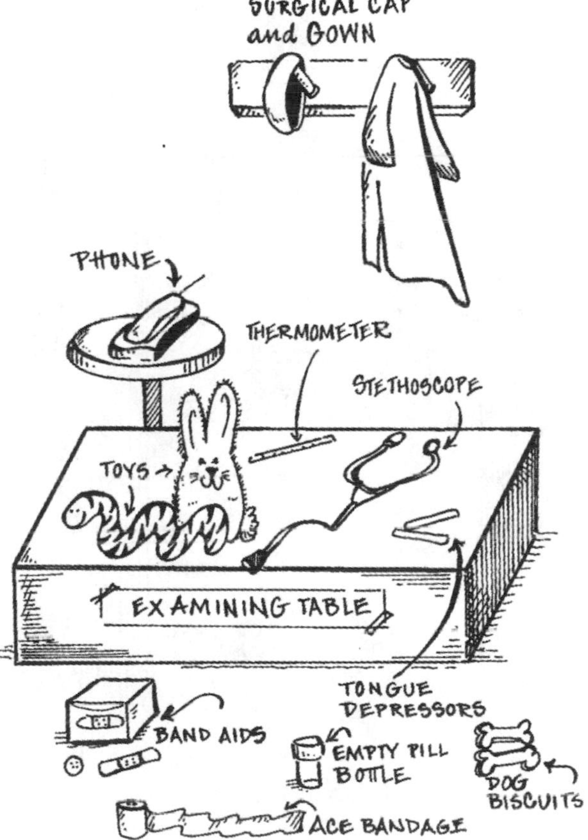

Let's Play Astronaut

OUTER SPACE IS AS NEAR AS THE MOON, OR AS FAR AS THE IMAGINATION CAN TRAVEL. AND ANYTHING GOES IN OUTER SPACE!

The Basics

appliance box cut apart to stand like scenery (see illustration)
anything covered with aluminum foil (blocks, kitchen utensils, toys)
paper grocery bag helmets (cut to just past the ears)
art materials for making helmets, control, panel, space suits
crayons, markers, glue, tape, stapler, hole punch, scissors
control panel for rocket ship, made with a few of the following materials
aluminum foil • bottle caps • bubble wrap • large sheet of cardboard for panel
milk jug lids • old head sets • old microphone • orange juice caps
telephone cords, curly spirals • telephone wire from scrap cable (colored)
working computer, or discarded monitor

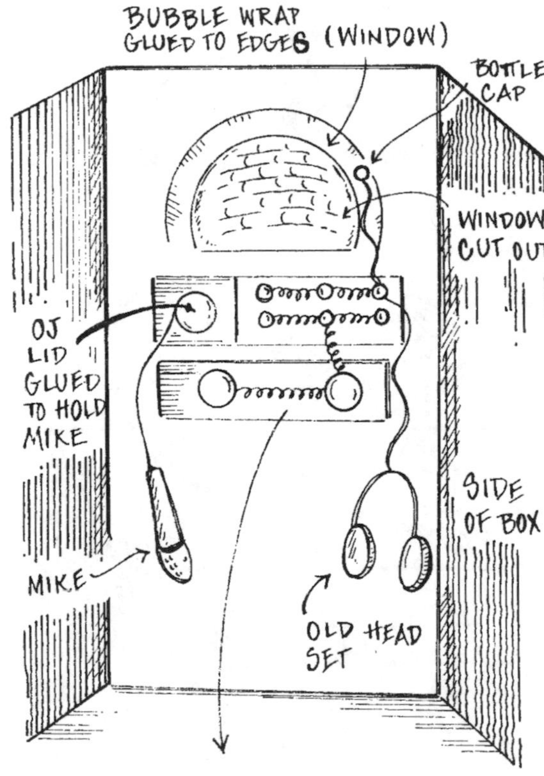

Steps

- Cut apart an appliance box and stand it up to make a small room that will be the rocket ship.
- Use art supplies to build a control panel with lots of buttons, knobs, dials, screens, and wires. Glue, tape, and staple them to a sheet of cardboard on the table.
- Wrap anything in aluminum foil, including the astronauts' arms and legs, to enhance space play. Make helmets and space suits from materials on hand.
- Now blast off for outer space! Everything is A-OK.

More Ideas

Paint with bubble wrap, pressing it on paper. It looks like moon craters.
Tack up pictures on the scenery to resemble windows in the rocket and what is seen from the ship as it flies through space.

Additional Materials

pictures of planets and outer space tacked to the walls around the control panel
choices of astronaut space suit parts and pieces
boots • cereal box jet pack • gloves • goggles • hose scraps as space suit gear
milk jug helmets (cut to fit) • potato chip can or oatmeal box air tanks • telescopes made from paper towel tubes

Let's Play Fast-Food Restaurant

Playing make-believe with fast food is an easy, energetic pretend activity enjoyed by a wide range of ages.

The Basics

table and chairs (eating area)
fast food supplies donated for play (start with one or two)
drinking straws • empty milk cartons • medium paper lunch sacks • paper cups with lids
paper plates • plastic silverware • small wax paper sandwich/fry bags
Styrofoam hamburger containers • wax paper squares

NOTE: FOR HEALTH AND SAFETY REASONS, DO NOT REUSE STRAWS AND SILVERWARE. REUSE PAPER AND CONTAINERS AGAIN AND AGAIN.

play food, handmade (start with two or three)
cardboard circles for onion rings • cardboard French fries • cardboard hamburger patties
cardboard hot dogs • cardboard pickles • cardboard tomato • chopped paper onions
plastic or paper cheese slice • shredded paper lettuce • Styrofoam buns and bread
art material, such as
cardboard • paper • markers • scissors • tape • glue

Steps

- Set up the restaurant.
- Decide on the roles to play, such as cook, order taker, customer, and janitor. Then pretend to be those people taking orders, cooking, cleaning, and buying and eating.
- Set up an assembly line of food preparation, cooking, and delivery, if desired.
- Trade jobs with friends and play all over again.

Additional Materials

restaurant sign and menu, including prices of food items, optional
choices of other restaurant items
napkins • paper hats for employees • small trays • play paper money and coins
empty mustard and ketchup bottles • plastic play food • trash can
note pads and pencils for orders
restaurant supply and machines made from cardboard boxes, such as
cash register • grill or stove area • ice machine • milk shake machine

Cooking, Games & Other Activities Too Fun to Miss

Chapter 7

Worms in the Dirt
I Know Somebody Who Swallowed a Fly
Moon Rocks
Mini-Mint Party Burgers
Painted Butterfly Snack
Stuffy Toy Talk
Edible Goldfish Aquarium
Flower Munching
Sweet Little Bird Nest
Sticky Cracker Cottage
For Always Sand Castle
Silly Antics
It's My Job!
Four Seasons Talk
Spinning Feelings

1 Worms in the Dirt

Children enjoy making believe they are eating "worms" pulled from a flower pot filled with "dirt." Very silly, very funny, and tastes good too.

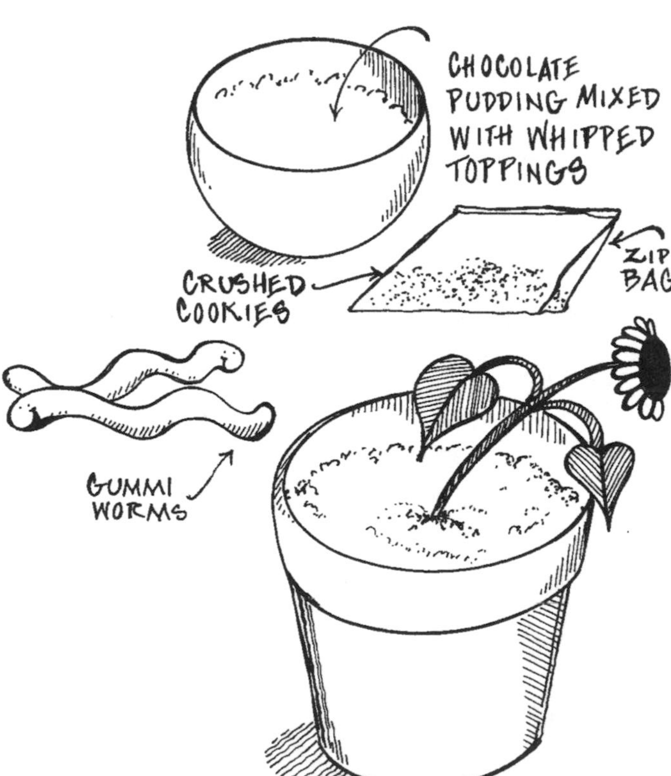

Materials

INGREDIENTS PER CHILD

½ cup (120 ml) whipped topping or whipping cream
½ cup (120 ml) chocolate pudding
3 chocolate sandwich cookies, such as Oreos, crushed in a resealable baggie
1 or 2 Gummi worms
small clean flower pot (cover the hole with a paper circle); paper or plastic cup; or small, clean milk carton
bowl
spoon
plastic flower, optional

Steps

- To make the "dirt," mix the whipped topping and chocolate pudding together in a small bowl.
- Place two chocolate sandwich cookies into a resealable baggie and crush them by hand. Pound and crush gently but firmly.
- Save a tablespoon or so of the crushed cookies for later. Pour the rest of the crushed cookies into the dirt mixture and mix.
- Scoop the dirt mixture into the clean flower pot. As a flower pot substitution, use a paper cup, a plastic cup, or a clean milk carton.
- Push the Gummi worms into the dirt.
- Sprinkle the top of the dirt with more crushed cookies to look like potting soil.
- Insert a clean plastic flower, for fun, if desired.
- Eat the dirt, and don't be too surprised to find that worm in the pot!

I Know Somebody Who Swallowed a Fly

THERE WAS AN OLD LADY WHO SWALLOWED A FLY, AND NO DOUBT SHE WOULD PREFER THIS FLY THE NEXT TIME SHE'S HUNGRY. EATING A FLY IS A THRILLING AND SILLY MAKE-BELIEVE ACTIVITY FOR A REAL SNACK TIME.

Materials

FOR EACH FLY

1 chocolate sandwich cookie, such as Oreo
1 miniature chocolate sandwich cookie
6 thin pretzel sticks (or chow mein noodles)
chocolate frosting, for glue
2 red hot candies
2 wings, cut from wax paper
scissors
paper plate
plastic knife

Steps

- On a plate, assemble an edible fly using frosting as glue. Begin with a large chocolate sandwich cookie for the fly's body, and a small chocolate sandwich cookie for the fly's head.
- Add pretzel sticks for legs.
- Add red-hot candies for eyes.
- Cut paper wings from wax paper and stick to the fly's body.
- Sing the song, "I Know an Old Lady Who Swallowed a Fly" and eat the fly cookie snack (leave the wings on the plate).

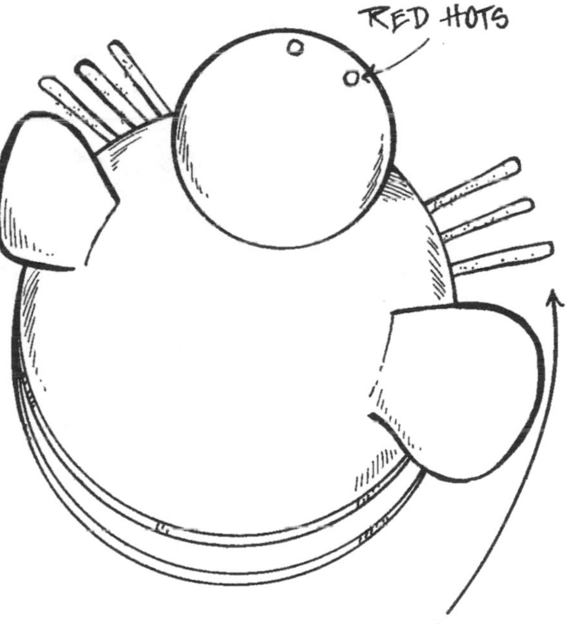

More Ideas

Create a spider with one cookie and chow mein noodles for legs.

Moon Rocks

Ever been to the moon? No? Moon Rocks will make you think you've just visited the moon and collected samples to bring back to earth.

Recipe halves, doubles, or triples nicely.
Makes at least 8 moon rocks.

Materials

2 cups (480 ml) peanut butter
bowl
1⅓ cups (320 ml) honey
clean hands for mixing
2 cups (480 ml) raisins
resealable baggie
2 cups (480 ml) nonfat dry milk
wax paper on a cookie sheet
3½ cups (840 ml) crushed graham crackers
paper plates

Steps

- Mix the dry milk, raisins, and 3 cups (720 ml) of graham cracker crumbs in a bowl.
- Place the remaining ½ cup (120 ml) graham cracker crumbs in a baggie and set aside.
- Add the honey and peanut butter to the mixture in the bowl.
- Mix well by hand.
- Roll the mixture into small balls.
- Drop each ball into the baggie with the remaining graham cracker crumbs and shake to coat, making each one look like a moon rock.
- Place the coated rock on the wax paper on the cookie sheet.
- When all of the rocks are ready, eat and enjoy. They taste great with a cold glass of milk, just like the astronauts drink. And these pretend moon rocks are easier to chew than the real thing, too!

More Ideas

Substitute dried fruit bits for the raisins.
Crunchy or plain peanut butter work equally well.
Experiment forming shapes other than round balls as this dough can be shaped and molded easily.

Mini-Mint Party Burgers

Made vanilla wafers and peppermint patties, this is a party burger of the sweetest kind! Recipe makes ten to twenty burgers.

Materials

few drops of water
1 drop green food coloring
small, screw-top jar
¼ cup (60 ml) flaked coconut
cookie sheet
48 vanilla wafers
sesame seeds or poppy seeds
small, clean paintbrush or pastry brush
24 chocolate-covered peppermint patties, the small kind (same size as vanilla wafers)
oven preheated to 350°F (180°C)

Steps

- In a small jar, combine the drops of water with the green food coloring. Add flaked coconut. Put the lid on the jar and shake until the coconut is tinted green to resemble lettuce.
- Place 24 vanilla wafers flat side up on an ungreased cookie sheet.
- Top each wafer with a chocolate-covered peppermint patty.
- Bake the wafers until the chocolate begins to soften. This takes only a few minutes. Then remove them from the oven.
- Take a pinch of the green coconut and place it on a baked wafer. Do the same for all the other baked wafers.
- Top each wafer with another vanilla wafer, round side up, and press gently.
- With a clean paintbrush, pastry brush, or finger, brush the top vanilla wafers with just enough water to moisten so the sesame seeds or poppy seeds will stick. Sprinkle a few poppy seeds on each cookie.
- Serve as a party snack for people or pretend burgers for dolls and stuffed bears.

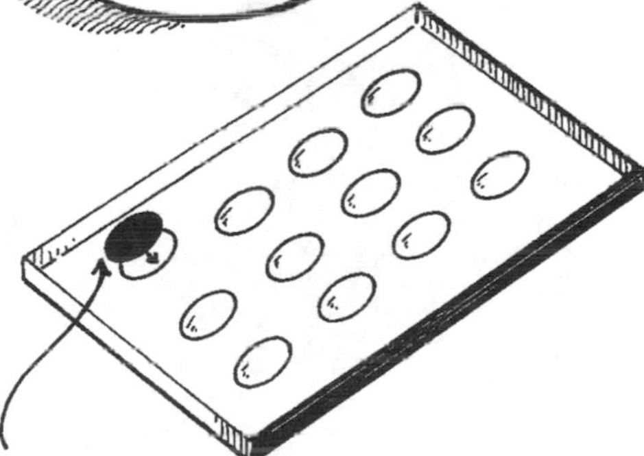

More Ideas

Add red colored frosting to the top "bun" before putting it on the "burger" to resemble ketchup. Do the same with yellow frosting for mustard, and white frosting for mayonnaise.
Add a square of yellow fruit leather to resemble cheese.
Serve as an April Fool's Day celebration snack or a special tea party treat!

Painted Butterfly Snack

Create bagel butterflies decorated with edible colored cream cheese.

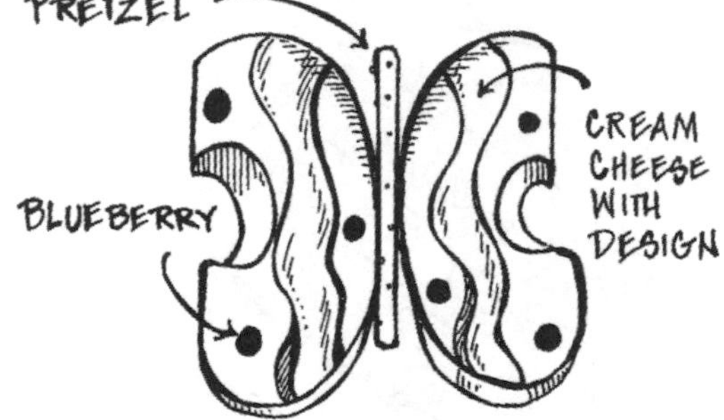

CUT IN HALF and PLACE AS ABOVE (BACK TO BACK)

Materials

one bagel for each butterfly
cream cheese
food coloring
foods or juices to color and flavor the cream cheese, such as
blueberries, crushed • brown sugar • chopped olives • chopped parsley • cinnamon
grape juice • jams or jellies • mashed strawberries • mustard • orange juice
pesto • salmon, smoked • salsa • shredded cheese • vanilla extract • vegetable juice, such as V-8
small cups
tongue depressors or popsicle sticks for each cup
plates
pretzel sticks
knife to cut bagel (adult only)

Steps

- Cut a bagel in half, making two half circles. Place on the plate. Rotate the circles so the curved sides touch. Set aside.
- Scoop a little cream cheese into each small cup; a tablespoon or two per cup is fine. Mix choices of foods, flavorings, or juices into each cup of cream cheese to make "flavored paint" to decorate the butterfly wings. Start with two or three.
- Spread the paint on the butterfly wings in any design imagined. Colors can be also be mixed as they are spread.
- Place a pretzel stick between the bagel halves in the center for the butterfly's body.
- Pretending can be a tasty experience!

Stuffy Toy Talk

1 ★

Bring stuffed toy bears, miniature beanbag animals, bunnies, and dolls to a carpeted area for some dialogue. Costume them in doll clothes and crazy accessories, or bring them as they are.

Materials

stuffed toys
costumes and accessories, optional, such as
brush/comb • crayon/paper • doll clothes • flowers • hat • ribbon, bow
silverware
tea cup
toy glasses

Steps

- Bring favorite toys—toy bears, bunnies, beanbag animals, dolls of all kinds, any toys large and small—to a carpeted area.
- Bring doll clothes, costume materials, or accessories and props to motivate acting possibilities. Or bring the toys as they are.
- To play Stuffy Toy Talk, place all the toys in the middle of the circle. All the players sit around the circle, leaving ample room between each.
- The first player chooses a toy from the pile. The object of the game is to begin a two-way conversation or dialogue with the toy, using different voices if desired. Tell a story, or chat about the day's happenings. Let the props help motivate talking.
- When done, the next player has a turn. Each player is welcome to use any toy in the pile, even if already used by another player.
- There are no winners in this game—just players.

More Ideas

Two children can work on a dialogue together without toys, using props or costumes, or chatting without them.
The child can engage more than one toy in the dialogue.
Put the toys in a box or behind a curtain. Reach in and pull out a surprise toy for an unplanned, natural, yet surprise conversation.

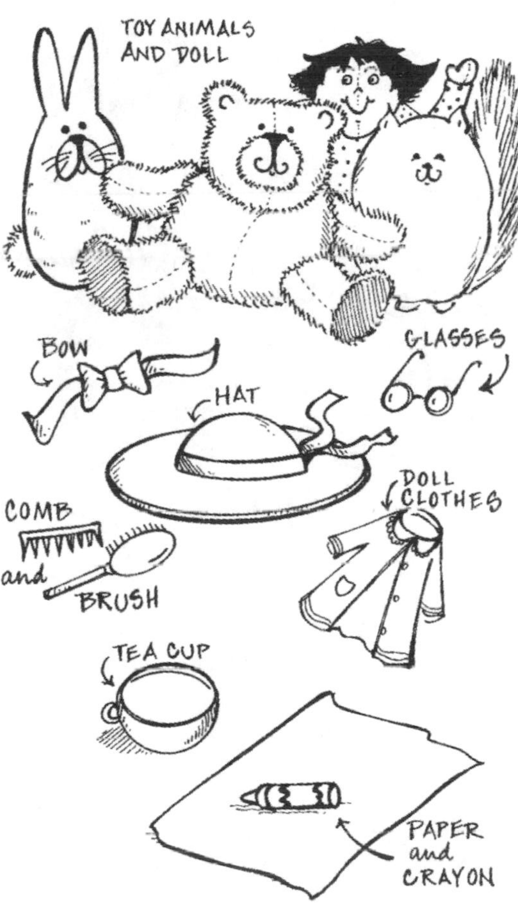

Edible Goldfish Aquarium

Let imaginations run wild as you add undersea delights to this edible aquarium.

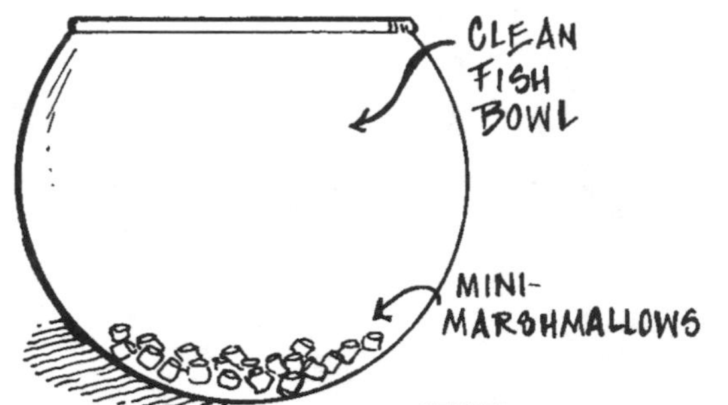

Materials

clean fish bowl (or other deep bowl)
colored mini-marshmallows
bowl and spoon
white grape gelatin, 3 oz. (90 g) package
ginger ale
blue food coloring
refrigerator
parsley sprigs, optional
mandarin oranges
Gummi worms, optional
star fruit, sliced, optional
measuring cups
The Five Chinese Brothers by Claire H. Bishop

Steps

- Start with a completely clean fish bowl. Cover the bottom of the bowl with mini-marshmallows.
- In a mixing bowl, prepare a 3 oz. (90 g) package of white grape gelatin with ginger ale (instead of water), following the package directions.
- Add a small drop of blue food coloring to turn the gelatin sea-green.
- Chill the gelatin, checking it and stirring it often until it has a thick jelly-like consistency.
- Spoon the gelatin over the mini-marshmallows in the fish bowl until they are covered.
- If desired, add a few sprigs of parsley to resemble seaweed, then more gelatin.
- Next add mandarin orange sections to resemble goldfish, then more gelatin on top of that.
- At this time, if desired, add Gummi worms and slices of star fruit to resemble eels and starfish. Continue adding gelatin and goldfish, eels, and starfish until the fish bowl is full.
- Chill until ready to serve. Gobble up a bowl full of ocean, then read *The Five Chinese Brothers* by Claire H. Bishop (New York: Putnam, 1996).

Flower Munching

PRETEND TO BE A HUNGRY LITTLE CATERPILLAR AND GOBBLE UP EDIBLE FLOWERS CRYSTALLIZED WITH DRIED EGG WHITES AND WATER. A BEAUTIFUL EXPERIENCE RIGHT ON THE BOUNDARY OF REALITY AND MAKE-BELIEVE.

Materials

edible flowers, such as several listed here

apple blossom • geranium • lilac • nasturtium • pansy • rose
tuberous begonia • viola • sesame seeds or poppy seeds • violet

NOTE: EDIBLE FLOWERS CAN REGULARLY BE FOUND IN LARGE GROCERY STORES IN THE PRODUCE DEPARTMENT. IF NOT, FLOWERS CAN BE PICKED FROM YOUR OWN YARD. BEST PICKED IN THE EARLY MORNING WHEN FRESH AND LIVELY LOOKING. BE SURE THAT ALL FLOWERS ARE CLEAN AND FREE FROM ANY CHEMICAL SPRAY.

¼ cup dried, powdered egg whites (available in bakery departments, cake decorating departments, or gourmet shops)

¼ cup (60 ml) warm water

whisk
cookie sheet
wax paper
small paintbrush
small bowl
granulated sugar

Steps

- Mix the dried egg whites and the warm water in a bowl with a whisk. Whisk for about two minutes, or until the powder is completely absorbed. Now whip the mixture until it is foamy and completely dissolved.
- Spread the blossoms out on a sheet of wax paper on a cookie sheet. They should have space between them and not touch. Petals can be plucked from blossoms and spread out individually for a daintier meal.
- Dip a small clean paintbrush into the egg white mixture and gently coat the blossoms. A thin coat is all that is needed.
- Next, sprinkle a little granulated sugar over the wet blossom. Follow the same steps with the other edible flower blossoms. Dry overnight.
- When dry, decorate cakes, sandwiches, salads, appetizers, snacks, or simply nibble like a deer, lizard, caterpillar, or fairy queen might do. But just eat the blossoms, not the stems.

NOTE: FLOWERS CAN BE MADE SEVERAL DAYS AHEAD. THEY STORE WELL IN AIRTIGHT CONTAINERS.

For information about edible flowers

- information@gourmetgardener.com
- www.northcoast.com/~alden/flowers.html
- *Tips for the Lazy Gardener* by Linda Tilgner
- *Flowers in the Kitchen: A Bouqet of Tasty Recipes* by Susan Belsinger

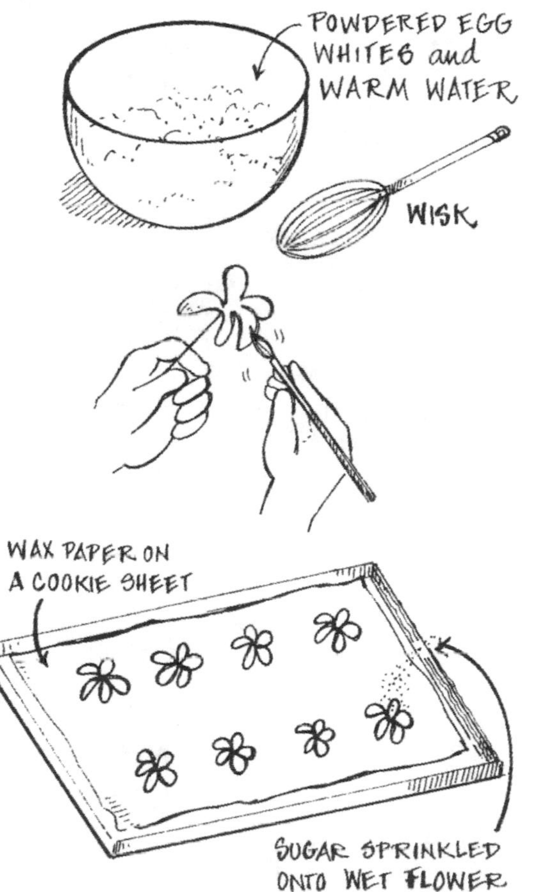

★★ 1

Sweet Little Bird Nest

Imaginative cooks prepare bird nests from shredded wheat and honey, each complete with a fruity inhabitant. Deliciously pretend!

Materials

paper muffin cup for each nest
empty margarine container
covered table (sticky activity!)
spoon
tongue depressor or small spatula
knife

FOR EACH NEST
large shredded wheat biscuit
1 tablespoon sunflower seeds, shelled
1 tablespoon raisins or currants
1 tablespoon coconut, shredded
honey in squeeze container
3 grapes for "eggs"
1 teaspoon butter or margarine

FOR EACH BIRD
pitted prune
1 teaspoon cream cheese, softened
1 carrot slice

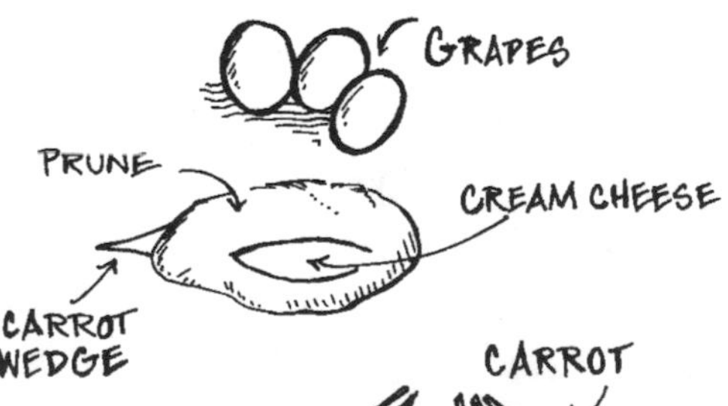

Steps

To make the nest

- Crumble the shredded wheat biscuit into the margarine container.
- Add sunflower seeds, raisins, and coconut.
- Squeeze a small amount of honey into the container and mix to make it all "stick" together.
- Scoop out the nest with the tongue depressor and place on a paper muffin cup liner. With buttered fingers, further shape the nest as desired.
- Place three grapes in the nest as pretend eggs.

To make the bird

- Cut the pitted prune, making a slit down one side.
- Stuff the prune with 1 teaspoon of softened cream cheese.
- Cut a ¼ wedge from the carrot slice. Press it into the cream cheese to resemble a beak.
- Place the rest of the carrot slice among the eggs in the nest. Stand the prune bird on the slice to resemble feet, using a little more cream cheese as glue if necessary.

Sticky Cracker Cottage

1 ★★

All you need for each of these houses is peanut butter, a small milk carton, and lots of little fun yummy decorations.

Materials

peanut butter
powdered sugar or nonfat dry milk, optional
bowl and spoon, optional
graham cracker squares
small milk cartons (one for each cottage)
spreading knife or craft sticks
yummy decorations, such as
  chocolate chips • coconut • dried fruit bits • mini-marshmallows • raisins • red hot candies
paper plate

Steps

- If desired, mix about a cup of peanut butter with a half cup of powdered sugar or nonfat dry milk. This will make the peanut butter less sticky and more manageable. Or, use the peanut butter straight from the jar.
- Place a clean, dry small milk carton on a paper plate. Spread peanut butter on one wall of the carton. Stick a graham cracker square to the milk carton. Do this for all four sides of the carton.
- Next add two crackers for a roof in a tent fashion with peanut butter used for glue. Spread the flat roof sides with peanut butter too.
- Now add decorations on the little cottage with more peanut butter as necessary. Use mini-marshmallows, red hot candies, raisins, coconut, or other candies and fruits for decorations. Sifted powdered sugar makes a nice touch too.
- Eat the cottage after enjoying it as a decoration.

More Ideas

Build a village of cottages on a table. First cover the table with wax paper for easy clean-up.
Add little toys or figures to each cottage.
Add other scenery decorations like toy cars, horses, trees, or pets.

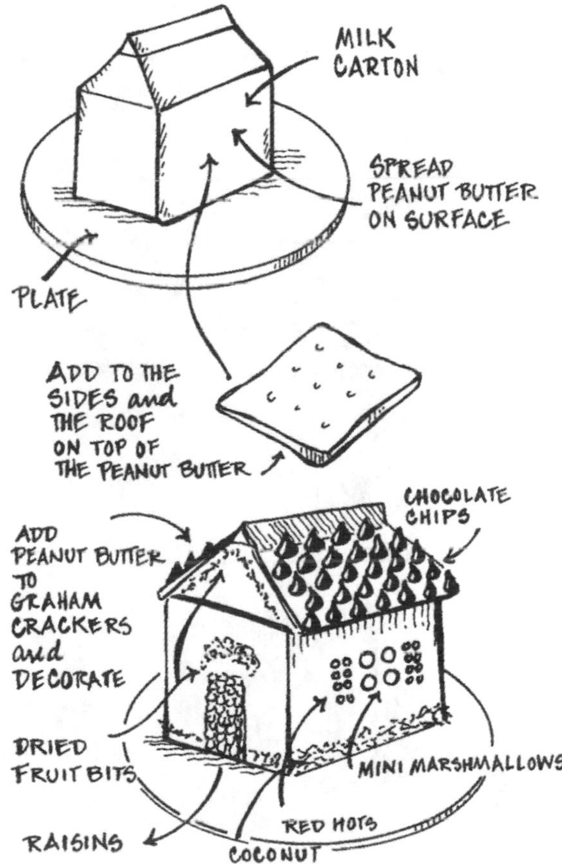

★★ 1

For Always Sand Castle

Building sand castles with wet sand is an imaginative activity leading to lots of pretend and make-believe. How wonderful to build a sand castle that can be saved instead of washed into the sea!

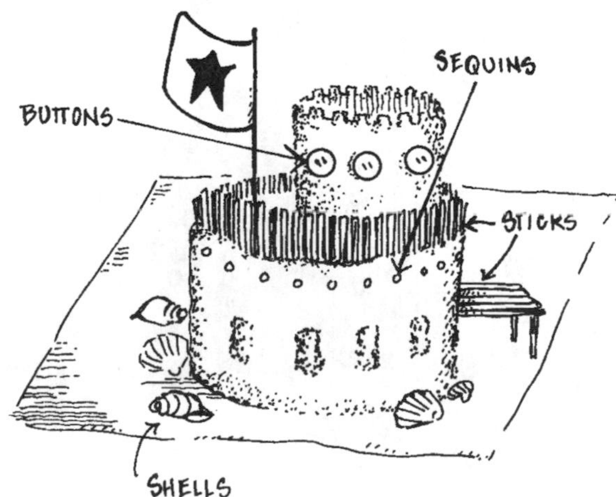

Materials

The Paste Mixture
1/3 cup (80 ml) flour
2 tablespoons sugar
1 cup (240 ml) water
1/3 teaspoon oil of cinnamon, optional

The Castle Recipe
6 cups (1.5 L) sand
1 cup (240 ml) paste mixture
water
mixing bowl
mixing spoon

containers for building castle, such as
cans • cottage cheese cup • margarine cup • paint pot • paper cup • plastic cup
small bucket • Styrofoam cup • yogurt cup
heavy cardboard or piece of plywood for the base
spoon, knife, screw driver or other tool
optional decorations/collage materials, such as
beads • buttons • flags • sequins • shells • sticks
paints and brushes, optional

Steps

- First mix the paste mixture in the mixing bowl.
- Next mix six cups of sand with one cup of paste mixture. Now add water until the mixture is like clay. It should pack firmly into containers.
- Create a castle with the containers and the sand mixture on a plywood or cardboard base.
- Add sticks, flags, shells, buttons, or other decorations as desired.
- Cut windows with a spoon, knife, screwdriver, or other tool, or the castle can be left without windows.
- Let the castle dry at least overnight.
- When dry, paint the castle or leave as is.

More Ideas

Coat the castle with any clear acrylic hobby coating or spray it (adult only) with clear enamel in a well-ventilated area.

Silly Antics

THINK UP AND PERFORM SILLY ANTICS TO THE DELIGHT OF OTHERS IN THE GAME. THEN IT'S THEIR TURN! IT'S MAY BE EMBARRASSING, BUT THAT'S THE FUN OF IT!

Materials

2 or more friends
index cards
markers

Steps

- Make the Silly Cards by thinking up silly antics to write on each index card. A simple, clear drawing may be used instead of words, if desired. Some ideas are

  sing Mary Had A Little Lamb
  you are a tiny seed growing
  hop up and down on one foot
  dig a hole and jump in
  climb up Jack's beanstalk
  pretend you are asleep
  kiss your mother goodnight
  blink your eyes,
  stick out your tongue
  go swimming
  clap your hands, jump up and down
  swim in Jell-O
  cry like a little baby
  row, row, row your boat
  go fishing and catch a whale
  smile with your lips glued shut
  plant a flower
  sing any song all by yourself
  spin around 3 times, but don't fall
  take your fish for a walk

- Place the cards in a pile on the floor.
- To play the game: Sit beside the Silly Cards. The first player draws a card and must perform whatever the cards says. Now it's the next person's turn, and so on. Everyone performs the embarrassing, silly antics described on the cards. Laughing is required!

HOP UP AND DOWN ON ONE FOOT
CLIMB UP JACK'S BEANSTOCK
GO SWIMMING
ROW ROW YOUR BOAT

More Ideas

Spread out all the Silly Cards face up. One player chooses a specific card and gives it to the other person to act out. Now that person does the same for the next player, selecting a specific card for the first player to act out.

It's My Job!

CUT OUT PICTURES OF CAREERS AND JOBS. PASTE THEM ON CARDS FOR AN EASY ACTING GAME THAT HELPS CHILDREN EXPERIENCE BEING A GROWN UP! BE PREPARED FOR SILLINESS, AND LAUGHTER!

Materials

old magazines and catalogs
scissors
glue or paste
index cards or lightweight cardboard cut into index cards

Steps

- Cut out pictures of different jobs and careers from magazines or catalogs.
- Glue them on index cards. Dry.
- To play an acting game with the cards, place them face down on the floor. From one to eight players sit around the cards in a circle.
- Player one peeks at the card and then places it face down so no one else can see it. Then he acts or mimes what the job on the card is like to him. The others try to guess what job he is acting out. For example, if the player draws a card that says "SINGER," he acts with or without sound, miming, or pretending to be a singer. The others must guess.
- Then the card can be removed from the game and it's the next person's turn.

More Ideas for Playing the Game

Spread out all the cards and choose one to act out.
Hand a card to a friend and ask him to act it out.

JOB CARD SUGGESTIONS

acrobat • artist • astronaut • baker • baseball player • carpenter • cowboy • dancer
doctor • firefighter • flight attendant • gardener • ice skater • lion tamer • movie star
musician • photographer • pilot • plumber • sea captain • singer • sports star
teacher • truck driver • veterinarian • writer • zoo keeper

Four Season Toss

EXPERIENCE A JOURNEY ACTING OUT THE FOUR SEASONS BY TOSSING A PENNY ONTO ANY SQUARE ON THE PLAYING BOARD AND THEN ACTING IT OUT.

Materials

four sheets of poster board, one per season
permanent marker
markers, crayons, colored pencils
yardstick
clear contact paper to cover board
one penny per player
one to eight players

Steps

TO MAKE THE BOARDS—(one for each season)

- With a yardstick, measure and create lines to make twelve equal boxes. (More or less boxes will also work.) Draw the lines with a permanent marker.
- In each box, write or draw (or both) the following seasonal suggestions, or think up your own. See the illustrations for picture ideas.

NOTE: MAKE ONE BOARD AT THE BEGINNING OF EACH SEASON RATHER THAN ALL FOUR AT ONCE.

Fall Suggestions

CREAK like an old house
DRIVE like a school bus
FALL like a leaf
FLOAT like a ghost
FLY like a bat
HOOT like an owl
MOVE like the wind
SMILE like a jack-o-lantern
SWAY like a tree
TEACH like a teacher
TRICK or TREAT
VANISH like the moon

Winter Suggestions

BAKE like a cookie
CURL like a ribbon
FALL like a snowflake
FLY south like a bird
FREEZE like a pond
FROST like a window
HIBERNATE like a bear
MELT like a snowman
OPEN like a present
SHINE like a star
SING like an angel
SPIN like a skater

FLY SOUTH LIKE A BIRD
HOOT LIKE AN OWL
FALL LIKE A SNOWFLAKE
SWAY LIKE A TREE

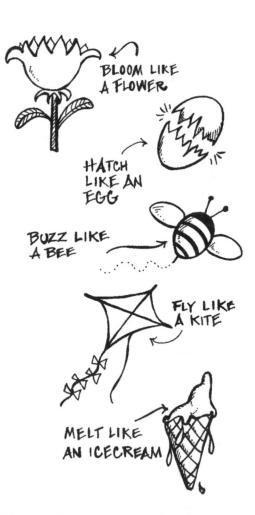

Spring Suggestions

ARCH like a rainbow
BLOOM like a flower
FLY like a kite
GROW like the grass
HATCH like an egg
HOP like a bunny
MOW like a lawnmower
OPEN like an umbrella
PLANT like a gardener
SPLASH like a puddle
SPRINKLE like the rain
WADDLE like a duck

Summer Suggestions

BURN like the pavement
BUZZ like a bee
EMPTY like a glass of water
FISH in a stream
FLOAT like a cloud
FLY like a baseball
HIKE up the mountain
JUMP in the pool
MELT like ice-cream
RACE like a motorboat
SHINE like the sun
SWIM like a fish

- Cover the board with clear contact paper to protect the drawings.

To play four season toss

- The players group around the board. The first player tosses a penny on the board. Whichever square it lands in, the player must act out. For example, if the square says, "MELT like a snowman," the player pretends to slowly melt into a puddle on the floor.

NOTE: ONE PLAYER CAN EFFECTIVELY PLAY ALONE OR WITH A FAVORITE STUFFED ANIMAL.

- Now it is the next person's turn. This player repeats tossing a penny on the board. If it lands on the same square as someone else's, that's fine–just act it out again. Everyone has different interpretations.
- Continue playing until everyone who wants to has had as many turns as they like or until time runs out.

More Ideas

For better storage of the large board, cut it in half or in fourths before covering with clear contact paper. Leave about 1/4″ (6 mm) between the sections and then cover with clear contact paper. The board will then fold up into halves or quarters.

This game could be made on cards to draw from a pile, or on a circular board with pie-shape sections and a spinner in the center.

Spinning Feelings

CONSTRUCT A SPINNER WITH FOUR FACES SHOWING THESE FEELINGS: HAPPY, SAD, SURPRISED, AND ANGRY. MAKE UP A FEW IMAGINARY SITUATIONS, AND ACT THEM OUT ACCORDING TO WHICH EMOTION THE SPINNER POINTS TO.

Materials

FOR THE SPINNER

- plastic coffee can lid
- heavy paper plate (circle)
- square of cardboard
- brad
- pencil
- scissors
- permanent markers
- index cards

Steps

Getting ready

- To construct the spinner: Cut an arrow from the plastic coffee can lid. Punch a hole in it with the points of a pair of scissors and set aside. Trace the paper plate with a pencil on a square of cardboard. Cut the cardboard 1″ to 2″ (5 cm to 10 cm) larger than the traced circle. Poke a hole through the center of the paper plate with a pencil point or scissors tips, and another hole through the center of the cardboard square. Join the plate and the square with a brad. To do this, push the brad through the plastic arrow, through the plate, through the cardboard, and open it to the back of the cardboard. Now spin the plate. If it does not spin, make the hole in the plate larger or loosen the brad a little.
- To make the feelings circle: Draw two lines crossing each other directly through the center of the plate to divide it into four equal pie shapes. First draw light pencil lines, and when happy with the lines, go over them with a permanent marker. In the first pie shape space, draw a happy face. In the next space, draw a sad face. Draw a surprised face and an angry face in the last two spaces. Other feelings faces could be drawn instead of any of these four, such as: sleepy, bored, goofy, giddy, dreamy, thrilled, or melancholy.
- To make the situation cards: With adult help, write situations that the child thinks up, such as any similar to the following:

  a goat is eating your shoes
  a space ship landed in your backyard
  it's lunch time
  nothing to eat but candy bears for breakfast, lunch, and dinner!
  telephone call for you
  two monsters are at your door

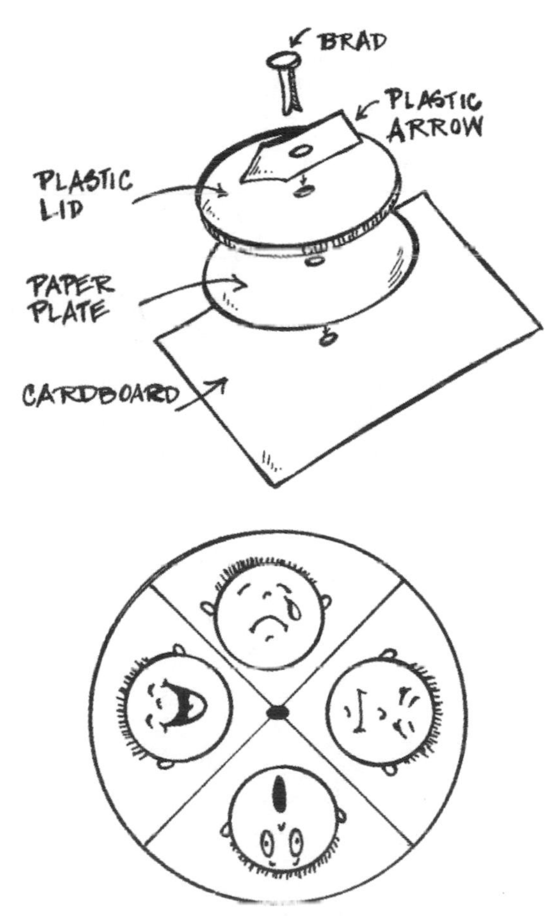

you are fishing in a stream
you are opening a birthday present
you can fly
you have a new puppy
your baby brother wants to be fed
your birthday cake is ready to eat!

Write one "situation" per card. A simple, clear picture can be drawn instead of writing, if desired. The game works best if the child helps think up the situations for the cards.

To play

- Any number of players (from 1 to 8) sit in a circle with the spinner and the situation cards in the middle of the circle.

NOTE: ONE CHILD CAN EFFECTIVELY PLAY THIS GAME WITH A STUFFED ANIMAL OR TOY.

- The first player draws a card, then spins the feelings spinner.
- The player must act out the situation using the emotion on the spinner. For example, if the player draws the "you just got a new puppy" card, and the spinner lands on "happy," the player acts out what it might be like to be happy about getting a new puppy, using happy words and saying happy things. But if the spinner says the player is sad about it, this changes the situation completely, and the player must act sad about getting a new puppy. Dialogue can be very important, or omitted entirely.
- The next player takes a turn. And so on.

More Ideas

Cut out magazine pictures and paste them on index cards for the situation cards to be acted out using different feelings on the spinner

Select a feeling, then act out a random or selected situation with the chosen feeling.

Select a feeling and a situation, and ask a friend to act it out.

Index

Materials Index

N

O

P

S

T

U

V

W

X, Y, Z

Icon Index

Beginner

Some experience

Experienced

Cooking

Cutting

Drawing

Game

Glue, Tape, etc.

Just hands

Painting

Sculpture

Sewing

Weaving

Materials likely to be found in the home or school

2 Familiar materials, but may need to be found or purchased

Materials may be unfamiliar, but easily gotten

Caution

Project Index

A

B

C